The United Nation

CRIME
PREVENTION

United Nations
NewYork,1996

Table of Contents

Introduction:
Seeking security and justice for all

The United Nations crime-fighting directorate was elevated in 1992 to the level of an intergovernmental Commission on Crime Prevention and Criminal Justice, at the request of the General Assembly and under the mandate of the Economic and Social Council (ECOSOC). The move reflects the seriousness with which the prevention of crime and the strengthening of criminal justice systems are regarded at the international level.

Domestic crime threatens the safety of citizens around the world and degrades once-proud centres of culture and commerce. In the international arena, organized crime syndicates as a group take in an estimated $1000 billion a year, and can outgun many national Governments and outbid them for the allegiance of public officials. Whether caused by bands of street toughs or sophisticated international organizations, crime poses a clear and present danger to harmonious and sustainable development. It misdirects economic activity, undercuts democracy and social solidarity and threatens the security of individuals and families.

Never has effective international cooperation against crime been so badly needed. Liberalization and globalization of markets and finances — combined with advanced technology applied to transport, communication and transfer of monies — are opening doors to transnational crime as well as to legitimate economic activity. Recent financial and currency crises indicate that the activities of what United Nations Secretary-General Boutros Boutros-Ghali terms "crime multinationals" are restricting the beneficial effects of the new global economy while exacerbating its de-stabilizing and predatory aspects. Traffic in addictive narcotics continues to expand, despite the best efforts of individual nations to seal off their borders or repress local production; formerly insular syndicates based in Europe, Asia, Africa and the Americas are entering into joint ventures; and ominous links between terrorist and crime groupings have come to light. Attempts to deal with the difficult issue of immigration policy are further confounded by cross-border traffic in illegal migrants. Reckless environmental destruction spans national borders and territorial waters with increasing frequency and has taken such alarming forms that it is now recognized as a crime against the world itself.

In addition to forging international cooperation, the United Nations helps countries bolster domestic criminal justice systems and learn from each other's experience. Agreements reached at the Commission on Crime Prevention and Criminal Justice and at UN Crime Congresses set standards for humanitarian, fair and efficient criminal justice systems, while technical assistance from the

United Nations has helped scores of countries improve the functioning of courts, police and correctional institutions. The work of the UN's criminal justice programme and the application of guidelines and standards have been especially crucial in El Salvador, Cambodia, Palestine and Haiti, which in recent years have faced the urgent need to rapidly build or reform criminal justice systems from the ground up.

Crime prevention and criminal justice issues have been a concern of the United Nations since its early days. In 1950, the Organization assumed global responsibility in the field by taking over the functions of the International Penal and Penitentiary Commission (IPPC), an intergovernmental organization established in the nineteenth century. Many changes have taken place in the crime prevention system since 1950, but the Commission and its secretariat, the Crime Prevention and Criminal Justice Division, continue to be enjoined by the United Nations Charter to promote "international cooperation in solving international problems of an economic, social, cultural or humanitarian character" and by the United Nations Declaration of Human Rights to support the "right to life, liberty and security of person" for all.

The present publication contains an overview of this important area of work of the United Nations. Following the main text is a compendium of criminal justice guidelines and standards, published in abbreviated form. Full texts, and more information about technical assistance programmes, may be obtained from:

United Nations Crime Prevention and
Criminal Justice Division
United Nations Office at Vienna
Room E1233
P.O. Box 500
A-1400 Vienna, Austria
Tel.: 43-1-21-345-4269
Fax: 43-1-21-345-5898
Cable address: UNATIONS VIENNA
Telex: 135612
E-mail: aboulouk@unov.or.at

Chapter 1

A Short History of International Cooperation Against Crime

Systems of criminal justice have been in existence since the dawn of human civilization. Clay tablets from 2400 B.C. listing a code of conduct were unearthed at an archaeological site in Syria. A more elaborate set of laws was developed in the twenty-first century B.C. under the Third Dynasty of Ur in ancient Sumeria, eventually to be superseded by the Code of Hammurabi of the seventeenth century B.C.

In many places in the world for much of the span of history, however, criminal justice was handled more informally. An assault on the person or on the rights of an individual was often regarded as a private matter, to be settled by the contending parties or their families. Violations of political authority or social or religious norms frequently resulted in wholesale sanctions against a tribe, kinship network or commune. Customary mechanisms for resolving disputes exist even today in some areas of the world, especially Africa, based on restitution and the restoration of social harmony rather than an adversarial courtroom procedure.

Outlaws

Exile was a commonly used sanction for serious offences. The offending party or parties were driven away from the community, stripped of their rights and deprived of the support of their kin. Exile was among the social mechanisms that led to the existence of the outlaw—someone living outside the bounds of legal convention. Outlawed individuals tended to join together in bands that provided their own rugged forms of mutual protection and regulation of rights. Out of necessity, they based themselves at the fringes of the settled portions of the world. Bandits took to the hills and mountains, swamps and jungles; buccaneers flying their own flags plied the high seas and ruled over isolated islands. Banishment and exile continued into relatively modern times, and were even linked to colonial settlements from European nations in North America and Australia.

Outlawry has provided the world with an array of colourful figures, celebrated in lore and legend. The reputations of selected brigands were enhanced by the perception that they had been outlawed due to political persecution or the skewed workings of a biased system of justice. But for every Robin Hood who may have stolen from the rich and given to the poor, there were a greater number who preyed on the defenceless for their own enrichment. Certainly, those who were victimized failed to appreciate the swashbuckling charisma of outlaw leaders. More generalized social costs were exacted by the restrictive effect of brigandage on travel and commerce.

Outlaws continue to operate in the contemporary world, and they still take advantage of isolated terrain. Processors and traffickers of illicit drugs maintain base areas in the mountains and rain forests, and pirates of a sort prey on shipping and smuggle illegal aliens. The range of organized crime, however, has been extended in recent times to include sophisticated networks operating at the heart of the big cities. The sale of addictive drugs, fencing of stolen goods, illegal gambling, prostitution, extortion and loan sharking are run as business ventures, and public officials routinely are corrupted. Criminal groups operating on a large scale and reaping tremendous profits are able to utilize the latest technology and mimic military and corporate organizational structures. In many cases, their capabilities outstrip those of the forces of social control.

Criminal justice at the international level

The growth in recent centuries of national States and national Governments, with their own sub-levels of localized authority, brought increasingly sophisticated codification of laws pertaining to criminal behaviour. Large-scale systems comprising police forces, courts and prisons were appearing in the major cities by the nineteenth century.

The implementation of international guidelines for criminal justice, however, is at a more tentative stage.

The effort is not without precedent. Roman law was applied within an empire that covered most of Europe and parts of Africa and West Asia. Regulation of social conduct incorporated in Islamic law spread to lands spanning three continents and continues to serve as an important element of the judicial systems of many countries. The Declaration of the Rights of Man encapsulated the ideals of the French Revolution and attempted to formulate universal standards for the protection of individuals and property. But these systems grew from particular political regimes and cultural conventions, and lacked the worldwide consensus required of a truly international approach to the control and prevention of crime.

One of the earliest forms of cooperation between sovereign nations in the field of law enforcement involved efforts to control piracy on the high seas — but this effort was often undercut by the practice of rival nations chartering freelance privateers to harass their rivals.

In the nineteenth century, scientific and pseudo-scientific studies of the causes of crime and the proliferation of reformatories and penal institutions drew widespread attention to the field of criminology. A series of conferences in Europe, of which the most notable was the First International Congress on the Prevention and Repression of Crime, in London in 1872, brought together experts and professionals from various countries. Leading issues under consideration included the proper administration of prisons, possible alternatives to imprisonment, modes of rehabilitating convicted criminals, treatment of juvenile offenders, extradition treaties and the "means of repressing criminal capitalists".

At the close of the London Congress, the International Prison Commission (IPC) was formed, with a mandate to collect penitentiary statistics, encourage penal reform and convene ongoing international conferences.

The formation of the League of Nations in 1919 and the Permanent Court of International Justice (popularly known as the World Court) in 1920 broke new ground in establishing standards of international justice. Galvanized by the breakdown of international order that led to the First World War, the founders of the League sought to regulate the conduct of States in a manner roughly analogous to the regulation of individual behaviour by criminal and civil law. The IPC established an affiliation with the League of Nations and held conferences in European capitals every five years between 1925 and 1935. At the last of this series of conferences, it was renamed the International Penal and Penitentiary Commission, or IPPC.

Enter the United Nations

The League of Nations foundered on the rocks of global conflict culminating in the Second World War, and so did the IPPC. When the United Nations was formed after the close of the war, it was decided that the control and prevention of crime would be included in its brief. The Organization declined, however, to accept affiliation with the IPPC, and for understandable reasons. Seventy-five years of valuable work and collection of research materials were tarnished by the Commission's 1935 conference, held in Berlin and dominated by adherents of the Nazi Government in power in Germany. During the war years a substantial part of funding for the IPPC came from the Axis powers, and the Commission all too frequently served as a publicist for theories on the racial and biological roots of crime and draconian measures for its control.

General Assembly resolution 415 (V) of 1 December 1950 dissolved the IPPC while incorporating its functions and archives within the operations of the United Nations.

From the beginning, United Nations involvement in crime prevention was seen as extending beyond the day-to-day contest between criminals and law enforcement agencies.

The United Nations Temporary Social Commission took the position that the prevention of crime and the treatment of offenders affected the fabric of society, and therefore were matters for social policy, and the UN's mandate to assist in improving criminal justice systems was linked to the Charter of the United Nations and the Universal Declaration of Human Rights. In the Preamble to the Charter are commitments to:

> reaffirm faith in fundamental human rights, in the dignity and worth of the human person . . . , to promote social progress and better standards of life in larger freedom, and for these ends . . . to employ international machinery for the promotion of the economic and social advancement of all peoples.

Article I of the Charter defines one of the four basic purposes of the United Nations as that of achieving

> international co-operation in solving international problems of an economic, social, cultural or humanitarian character, and in promoting and encouraging respect for human rights and for fundamental freedoms for all without distinction as to race, sex, language or religion.

Article 28 of the Declaration of Human Rights states that "everyone is entitled to a social and international order in which the rights and freedoms set forth in this Declaration can be fully realized". Among these rights are, according to Article 3, the "right to life, liberty and security of person". Article 12 provides: "No one shall be subjected to arbitrary interference with his privacy, family, home or correspondence, nor to attacks upon his honour and reputation. Everyone has the right to the protection of the law against such interference or attacks"; Article 17(2) adds that "No one shall be arbitrarily deprived of his property".

These provisions from the Declaration of Human Rights cut two ways. They posit the right of the people of the world to enjoy domestic tranquillity and security of person and property without the encroachment of criminal activity. At the same time, they predicate equitable systems of justice that protect citizens' rights and liberties.

The congresses and conferences of the United Nations reflected a growing awareness of the structural causes of crime and the need for measures to alleviate economic and social conditions that foster criminal behaviour. The corollary to this notion is awareness that crime is an impediment to viable economic and social development; that it diverts energies and resources from constructive endeavour, degrades individuals through various illicit activities such as drug trafficking and drug abuse, corruption and prostitution, places large sectors of economic activity outside the regulation of States and beyond the reach of tax collectors, and through corruption of public authorities undercuts the credibility and efficacy of Governments. The United Nations accordingly has promoted effective strategies for incorporating planning for crime prevention and criminal justice within overall social and economic development planning, as well as building and strengthening democratic institutions.

The United Nations was barely ten years old when the First United Nations Congress on the Prevention of Crime and the Treatment of Offenders was convened in 1955 at the Palais des Nations in Geneva. Bringing together government officials, law enforcement personnel, penologists, sociologists and criminal justice scholars, the Congress focused on two areas that were mainstays in the deliberations of the old IPPC and had taken on renewed significance: treatment of prisoners and juvenile delinquency.

Cruel and inhuman treatment of those held in the custody of criminal justice systems has been a blight on civilization throughout history, but was a particularly poignant issue in the aftermath of the Second World War, while memories of barbarities meted out in prisons and concentration camps were still fresh. Lawlessness among young people had grown to startling proportions in Europe during the years following the Second World War, spurred by the ravaged physical and social environment and high number of orphaned or abandoned children. To an unprecedented degree, anxiety about juvenile delinquency was reflected in a multitude of academic studies, novels, movies and television shows on the subject among the Western nations that dominated the early membership of the UN.

The 95 Standard Minimum Rules for the Treatment of Prisoners, drafted by the Congress and later approved by the Economic and Social Council (ECOSOC), have had a cumulative impact on the practices of Member States and also paved the way for future international criminal justice standards. Exploration of the problem of juvenile delinquency directed attention to social inadequacies, leading toward an international consensus on the relation between the causes and effects of crime.

In accord with resolution 415 (V), the United Nations continued the IPPC practice of convening congresses every five years. The Second through Ninth Congresses were held, respectively, in London in 1960, Stockholm in 1965, Kyoto in 1970, again in Geneva in 1975, Caracas in 1980, Milan in 1985, Havana in 1990 and Cairo in 1995 (see Chapter IV for summaries of each Congress). At these Congresses, the practice of drafting international guidelines such as the 95 Standard Minimum Rules was extended.

The instruments approved by the Crime Congresses generally follow one of two basic forms: approved standards for the operation of certain aspects of criminal justice systems, or model treaties setting out areas of bilateral cooperation between nations. In the Appendix to this publication are summaries of the major instruments to come out of the Crime Congresses.

An organized response to organized crime

In the final decade of the twentieth century, for the first time since pirates and buccaneers disrupted maritime trade in the mercantilist era, transboundary crime has become a matter of global concern.

Transational crime organizations now dominate illicit international trade in drugs, prostitution, transport of aliens, smuggled gems and valuable metals, counterfeit currency, weapons and stolen goods. With combined annual sales that dwarf the gross domestic product of most countries and profit rates that commonly reach 70 per cent, they are able to to amass assets more rapidly than major corporations or international financial institutions.

Similarly to their legal counterparts, crime multinationals diversify operations and investments, make use of modern technology and enter into cooperative ventures. They infiltrate government agencies and legitimate businesses and utilize the international banking system to launder and reinvest profits.

The far-reaching political, economic and social consequences of "crime as business" have been a concern of the United Nations since 1975, when the Fifth Crime Congress examined changes in the forms and dimensions of criminality, both transnational and national.

In 1988, the United Nations Convention against Illicit Traffic in Narcotic Drugs and Psychotropic Substances was adopted by a high-level international conference held in Vienna, Austria. This Convention is one of the most important internationally binding instruments aimed at combating one of the most lucrative activities of international crime — drug trafficking. Among the changes which States parties agree to work towards under this treaty are criminalization of money laundering and increased cooperation in extradition, mutual legal assistance and transfer of proceedings in criminal matters.

Two key conferences on international action against international crime were held under the auspices of the United Nations in 1994.

The International Conference on Preventing and Controlling Money Laundering and the Use of the Proceeds of Crime, organized by the International Scientific and Professional Advisory Council to the United Nations Crime Prevention and Criminal Justice Programme in cooperation with the Italian Government, took place in June in Courmayeur, Italy. Limitation of financial secrecy was called an "absolute sine qua non of serious money laundering control and of sincere international cooperation". Participants called for application of the "know your customer" rule advocated by some international bodies, particularly with respect to abolishing anonymous bearer accounts and to identifying the real party represented by a "nominee". They called for laws to require the reporting of suspicious transactions, and the expansion of existing reporting requirements to cover funds derived from a wider range of crimes.

The Conference also recommended that research be conducted to identify businesses which may be serving launderers and to determine the feasibility of extending present regulations beyond banking and financial institutions, with a view to preventing rather than simply attempting to prosecute money laundering.

The first ministerial-level global conference to concentrate exclusively on the challenge posed by crime multinationals was held in November of the same year, in Naples, Italy. The idea for a such a conference was first proposed in 1991 by Giovanni Falcone, a crusading Italian magistrate assassinated by the Mafia in 1992. His work and that of his colleagues is credited with sharply curtailing the national influence of Italian crime syndicates.

Noting that wide variations among criminal codes obstruct international cooperation and allow criminal organizations safe havens from which to operate, the 142 countries represented agreed on the value of "closer alignment of legislative texts concerning organized crime". The Naples Declaration also endorsed greater use of bilateral and multilateral agreements on extradition and exchange of witnesses and evidence; personnel exchanges between national law enforcement agencies; and international assistance to criminal justice systems in developing countries. States are urged to consider making money laundering a crime, whether or not an illegal origin of the funds can be proven; requiring greater transparency of banks and other financial enterprises; and establishing laws providing for the seizure of organized crime assets.

Although the provisions of the Naples Declaration are not binding, the exchange of views that occurred for the first time at a high level is a necessary prerequisite to overcoming centuries-old obstacles to international cooperation. These include differences in crime codes and criminal justice practices and sensitivities concerning national sovereignty. In addition, the Naples Conference mandated that Governments worldwide be asked their views on the advisability of creating a convention on transnational crime that would be legally binding.

An agenda for the twenty-first century

The urgent need for international cooperation against crime was prominently mentioned at the historic commemoration of the United Nations fiftieth anniversary, from 22 to 24 October 1995 at New York Headquarters. Among the suggestions made by the 128 heads of State or Government in attendance (and representatives of 177 nations in all) were the United States call for a declaration on international crime and citizen safety and proposals from Bolivia and Colombia for an international conference on narcotics abuse and trafficking.

The General Assembly's "Declaration on the Occasion of the Fiftieth Anniversary of the United Nations" (A/RES/50/6) stated that the nations of the world must "act together to defeat the threats to States and people posed by . . . transnational crime and the illicit trade in arms and the production and consumption of and trafficking in illicit drugs."

In addition to the realization that organized transnational crime poses a serious threat to world security, other relatively new concerns regarding crime have come to the attention of the international community and the public at large.

The proliferation of computers and computer networks expands the possiblities for fraud and money laundering. Illicit disposal of nuclear and other forms of toxic waste and negligence in large-scale transoceanic transport of petroleum are among the actions now perceived as crimes against the natural environment. Use of large-scale technologies in agriculture at times produces results which can be said to be criminal: confiscation of tribal lands, frustration of land reform efforts or poisoning of farm labourers by chemical insecticides. The world has come to see theft of cultural patrimony — objects of historical, religious or artistic value — as a matter of concern to national criminal justice systems and international bodies, rather than a high-spirited "Indiana Jones"- style venture. Trafficking in persons — whether adult or child prostitutes or illegal aliens destined for forced labour in sweatshops — exploits and degrades people, often taking lives, and exacerbates the difficulties inherent in establishing fair immigration policies. Violence against women, once overlooked when taking place within a family structure or behind closed doors, now is condemned widely, and its prevention has become a matter of urgent concern.

These are among the complex questions of criminal justice policy that face the international community in the 1990s and are likely to remain on the agenda into the twenty-first century.

A larger, overarching question involves locating a balance between the twin exigencies of crime control and justice. On the one hand, improvement is called for in protecting the rights of those accused or convicted of crimes, with the ultimate goal of eliminating arbitrary arrest and detention, corrupt or biased courts and brutal treatment of offenders held in the custody of criminal justice systems. On the other hand, recent United Nations congresses have stressed the rights of victims of crime to protection under the law and, in some situations, to redress or restitution. Effective law enforcement and a fair criminal justice system are a bulwark protecting the rights of people to a secure existence and to develop their economic and social potential. At the fulcrum of these two arms of policy action is crime prevention. The incorporation of countermeasures to criminal behaviour into social development programmes offers a long-term hope for bringing the scourge of crime under control.

Chapter 2
The Costs of Crime

United Nations statistics show a steady increase in criminal activity worldwide in the 1970s and 1980s and project continued growth through the 1990s. Although rates differ each year, crime increases on average by about 5 per cent a year, controlling for population growth.

The number of recorded crimes jumped from about 330 million in 1975 to nearly 400 million in 1980 and is estimated to have reached half a billion in 1990. Between 1970 and 1980 the number of reported frauds, thefts and homicides jumped dramatically, with the most striking increases taking place in the more developed nations. The worldwide incidence of assaults skyrocketed, from a little over 150 per 100,000 population in 1970 to nearly 400 per 100,000 population in 1990. So did the incidence of thefts, going from slightly over 1,000 per 100,000 to close to 3,500 per 100,000 in the same period. In one major industrialized nation, the number of violent crimes per 100,000 grew from 498 in 1978 to 610 in 1987.

The Third United Nations Survey of Crime Trends, released in 1990, shows that the numbers of intentional homicides per 100,000 population rose from 1 to 2.5 between 1975 and 1985 in the developing countries; in the developed countries, the incidence in the same period changed from less than 3 to more than 3.5. In the significant category of drug-related crimes, the rate per 100,000 worldwide rose from 60 in 1975 to over 160 in 1985. Results of the Third Survey are used to project an increase in the overall crime rate per 100,000 from 4,000 in 1985 to close to 8,000 in the year 2000 unless national and international efforts can stem or reverse the trend.

More recent data — from the Fourth United Nations Survey — show that within a group of comparable countries, the number of recorded crimes per capita increased by an average of 23 per cent from 1986 through 1990.

Another United Nations study — the International Crime (Victim) Survey, carrried out in the 1990s — also indicates growth in crime in the post-war period. Based on interviews with individuals representing a cross-section of the population of 50 countries on all inhabited continents, the first round of the study showed that more than half the urban population worldwide had been victimized by a crime at least once during the period 1988-1994. It also profiled regions of relatively high crime rates — Africa, Latin America and "New World" countries such as Canada, Australia and the United States — as well as regions of relatively low crime rates in Asia, Europe and West Asian and Arab countries.

The monetary costs of the operation of crime prevention and criminal justice systems are substantial. A United Nations survey released in 1990 shows that the more highly developed countries expend an average of 2 or 3 per cent of their budgets on crime control. In the developing countries, expenditure commonly runs from 9 to 14 per cent of national budgets. According to the Third United Nations Survey, the developed countries maintain about 225 police officers for every 100,000 population and about 20 per 100,000 to staff prisons. In developing countries, the corresponding figures are higher: more than 500 police and over 50 prison staff per 100,000 population.

Indirect costs of crime include the consequences borne by members of society who are not usually perceived as victims. These costs are difficult to quantify in monetary terms, but very real. There is, for example, the emotional pain suffered by relatives and friends of crime victims. Witnesses have to spend hours, days or even months involved in police investigations and in court proceedings. Consumers have to pay higher prices as a result of crimes directed at businesses. Property owners pay higher insurance premiums for the risks of theft, arson and other crimes. Enterprises unable to afford increased premiums are driven out of business or left vulnerable to catastrophic financial loss, and businesses and citizens incur costs of security systems. Tax evasion brings on higher taxation of honest citizens and shortchanges the social goals of towns and nations.

Crime discourages investment — in low-income urban neighborhoods of industrialized countries as well as in developing countries and countries in transition plagued by crime syndicates. It diverts capital from productive opportunities and into speculative, short-term enterprises and luxury spending, with spin-off effects that include corruption of public officials, extortion of legitimate businesses and ruined lives.

The ability of crime to distort economic activity is most dramatically apparent in the workings of giant transnational syndicates. Taking advantage of the globalization and liberalization of trade and finances in the 1990s, these groups now constitute a major force in the world economy, able to affect the destinies of countries at critical stages in their economic development.

A United Nations Development Programme study found that large-scale drug trafficking brings an inordinate amount of foreign exchange into drug-exporting countries, fuelling inflation, overvaluing domestic currencies and bringing down the return on exports. Production of goods for export is further discouraged by money laundering, which, according to the preliminary report of the investigation, "fosters contraband activity, often lowering the costs of goods smuggled; propitiates the underbilling of imports and the overbilling of exports; stimulates the flight of capital and induces mistrust of foreign investors, thus affecting the equilibrium between savings and investment, as well as legal employment generation". *The Economist* magazine points out, in a 1995 article, that "where the main purpose of investment is to launder drug money, the effect is often to crowd out legal businesses". This is because the main objective of the money launderers is to transform illicit money into legitimate assets; it is therefore in their interest to keep a business in operation, even if it sells goods or services below cost. Legitimate businesses cannot compete with prices set in this fashion.

Economic losses are compounded by the undercutting of political institutions. This occurs in an extreme form when terrorist groups or private armies operating under the flag of a political movement establish linkages with crime syndicates. In several countries, this trend is blurring the distinction between legitimate police and armed forces, on the one hand, and territory-controlling criminal gangs, and in many more countries it undercuts the rule of law and frustrates the efforts of legitimate public administration.

One particularly onerous side-effect of international crime and the trade in drugs is increased juvenile delinquency. The young are particularly vulnerable to the temptations of drugs; along with other dangers and lures presented by organized crime, drug abuse is a major factor promoting marginalization from society. Although some nations have reported no significant increase in juvenile lawlessness, many countries have, and they are found on several continents and among the most developed and less developed nations alike. An especially disturbing trend is the apparently earlier onset of delinquency; ages 13 and 14 are increasingly those when habitual drug use and criminal offences begin. Factors in addition to drug abuse and contact with organized crime that are indicated as contributing to delinquency include the breakup of traditional family structures; tumultuous social change or civil strife; instability brought on by migration from the countryside to the city; and high rates of unemployment among teenagers.

Crimes of violence are not limited to street assaults and gang warfare. A great many occur within domestic households, and the victims are almost always women and children. Physical abuse of women behind closed doors is an age-old problem, but one largely ignored as a societal concern or criminal justice issue until relatively recently. The roots of the problem are clearly structural, relating to ingrained notions about the lesser status of women as well as to stress brought on by psychological, social and economic pressures. It is clear that, in addition to efforts to alleviate the causes, legal mechanisms offering protection and compensation to women who are physically abused are of immediate importance.

The destruction that crime visits on women and children weakens the viability of family structures, which are already under pressure from rapid cultural change and the general withdrawal of public social services in the 1990s. The breakdown of families is one of the highest costs we pay for crime. It also has a pernicious multiplier effect, as the destabilization of families tends to perpetuate and promote criminal behaviour.

Chapter 3
The United Nations Crime Prevention System

The Commission on Crime Prevention and Criminal Justice

Since 1992, the policy-making body of the United Nations in the crime control field has been the Commission on Crime Prevention and Criminal Justice. Composed of representatives of 40 Governments, the Commission is a functional body of the Economic and Social Council. After the General Assembly itself, ECOSOC is the major legislative and policy-making organ of the United Nations.

The Commission is charged with developing, monitoring and reviewing the UN crime programme and mobilizing support for it among Member States. It is also expected to coordinate the crime prevention activities of other entities of the United Nations system, as well as those of the interregional and regional institutes on crime prevention and criminal justice, and to organize the United Nations Congresses on the Prevention of Crime and the Treatment of Offenders.

Priority areas mandated by ECOSOC when it established the Commission in 1992 are:

- International action to combat national and transnational crime, including organized crime, economic crime and money-laundering;

- Promoting the role of criminal law in the protection of the environment;

- Crime prevention in urban areas, including juvenile and violent criminality; and

- Improving the efficiency and fairness of criminal justice administration systems.

Aspects of these principal themes are selected for consideration at each annual session of the Commission, held at the United Nations Office at Vienna. In accordance with ECOSOC resolution 1992/22, the Commission is to review all the priority themes at its fifth session, in 1996.

The Commission also oversees provision of technical assistance to requesting Member States in areas where the crime prevention programme possesses substantive competence. In addition, a standing item on the Commission's agenda is promotion of the use and application of United Nations criminal justice standards and norms.

Implementation of policy set by the Commission is the responsibility of the Crime Prevention and Criminal Justice Division of the United Nations Secretariat (see below).

Organizational lineage of the Crime Commission

The predecessor of the Commission was the Committee on Crime Prevention and Control (CCPC). The CCPC in turn replaced the Ad Hoc Advisory Committee of Experts, created in 1950 by General Assembly resolution 415 (V). The purpose of that group of seven experts was defined as "devising and formulating programmes for study on an international basis and policies for international action in the field of the prevention of crime and the treatment of offenders". The work of the Committee was later placed on a more permanent basis, and the strengthened body was called the Advisory Committee of Experts on the Prevention of Crime and the Treatment of Offenders.

Replacement of the expert group by the CCPC took place in 1971, under the mandate of ECOSOC resolution 1584 (L). The founding of the CCPC was a response to the then recently completed 1970 Crime Congress in Kyoto, which had broadened substantially the scope of UN interest in criminal justice policy (see Chapter IV).

A later review of the United Nations crime prevention programme figured prominently on the agenda of the 1990 Congress in Havana. It revealed that all countries shared an urgent concern regarding the increase of crime and the appearance of new forms of organized criminality, and reaffirmed that the United Nations could and should play a larger role in combating crime and promoting international cooperation and that its presence at the forefront of international efforts is crucial.

The Congress review was facilitated by a CCPC report concluding that a programme adequate to the pressing needs of the contemporary world must assist countries in dealing with both national and transnational crime. The programme, the report said, should encompass all forms of assistance — from information exchange and joint research to technical cooperation and collaborative action. Further, the organizational structure and size of a revamped programme must measure up to its purposes and to the volume and importance of mandates entrusted to it. The Committee proposed that a major new entity should be created to consolidate UN responsibilites in the field of crime and justice. This new entity would coordinate related United Nations functions and facilitate the expansion of international cooperation in investigation, adjudication, sanctioning, enforcement, research and training.

The report also stressed the need for strong political support from Member States and for this political will to be cemented through a ministerial-level summit meeting. In addition, a comprehensive international instrument on crime prevention and criminal justice, possibly in the form of an international convention, was proposed as a means of mobilizing stronger international support and coordination.

On the recommendation of the Eighth Congress, the General Assembly adopted a resolution convening a Ministerial Meeting on the Creation of an Effective United Nations Crime Prevention and Criminal Justice Programme, to be preceded by an intergovernmental working group. The findings of the working group became the basis for the Ministerial Meeting's decisions on structure, content and means of implementing the new body.

The ministerial Summit concluded its meeting in Versailles, France, in November 1991 by recommending replacement of the CCPC with a new intergovernmental commission. A resolution adopted by the UN General Assembly later that year asked the Economic and Social Council to establish the Commission on Crime Prevention and Control and set forth a relevant Statement of Principles and Programme of Action.

The Crime Prevention and Criminal Justice Division

The Division is the Secretariat body within the United Nations system that implements policy decisions of the Commission, formulates policy options and coordinates crime prevention and criminal justice activities within the United Nations system and at the international level. This work includes cooperation with entities such as the International Drug Control Programme, the Centre for Human Rights, the Department of Development Support and Management Services and the Office of Legal Affairs.

The Division promotes the application and use of United Nations international instruments and resolutions in the field of crime prevention and control through public information activities, and works closely with Member States to facilitate their implementation.

Among its field activities, the Division (until 1996 known as the Crime Prevention and Criminal Justice Branch) provided technical assistance and advisory services in connection with UN missions in Cambodia, Somalia and the former Yugoslavia, including the development of a training course for civilian police components of peace-keeping operations. It prepared and published a handbook on criminal justice, human rights and humanitarian law standards for peace-keeping supervisors and contributed to the re-establishment of the police and criminal justice systems in Cambodia and Somalia.

The origin of the Crime Prevention and Criminal Justice Division is traceable to the Section of Social Defence, created short-ly after the establishment of the United Nations.

One of the first activities of the Section of Social Defence was to gather and compile official crime statistics from Member States. Later on, the Section was reorganized and renamed the Crime Prevention and Criminal Justice Section. In 1977, the Section was re-named the Crime Prevention and Criminal Justice Branch and placed under the direction of an Assistant Director, who reported to the Assistant Secretary-General of the Centre for Social Development and Humanitarian Affairs. After a subsequent restruc-turing of the economic and social sectors of the UN and the disso-lution of the Centre for Social Development and Humanitarian Affairs, the Branch was affiliated with the United Nations Office at Vienna (UNOV), under the direction of the UNOV Director-General, who serves at the level of Under-Secretary-General.

In 1995, the fiftieth session of the General Assembly approved elevation of the Branch to the status of a Division. This promotion came shortly after the commemoration of the fiftieth anniversary of the United Nations, attended by 128 heads of State or Government, at which prominent mention was made of the need for international cooperation to combat and prevent crime (see Chapter III).

Informational activities

The Division collects, systematizes, analyses and exchanges interna-tional crime statistics and information. At the core of this effort is a country-by-country survey of crime trends and crime prevention and criminal justice policies, conducted every two years. The Division also is asked to promote action-oriented research and to study new forms and dimensions of crime, especially transnational crime (see Chapter VI).

The Division issues two regular publications:

- The annual *International Review of Criminal Policy* informs the international community on current methods, techniques and approaches to criminal justice policy and practice. The Review is published in English, French, Russian and Spanish.

- The *Crime Prevention and Criminal Justice Newsletter* disseminates information on United Nations activities and policies within the criminal justice field and opens an avenue of feedback from experts and government officials. It has been published twice a year since 1980.

The Crime Prevention and Criminal Justice Division is expanding its informational capacities by turning onto the world-wide information superhighway. Since the early 1990s, it has been providing useful information from a variety of crime and criminal justice databases to hundreds of electronic users. Work is under way on a more comprehensive system — with the working title "On-Line Crime and Justice Clearinghouse" — which would expand the secretariat's Internet services and multiply the amount of criminal justice information available to Governments at minimal cost (see Chapter V).

The Division is also working to facilitate technical assistance that will help developing countries computerize their criminal justice systems; means of fulfilling this objective were explored in depth in Cairo at a Ninth Crime Congress workshop.

Chapter 4

United Nations Congresses on the Prevention of Crime and the Treatment of Offenders

The United Nations Crime Congresses bring together representatives of the world's national Governments, criminal justice professionals, scholars of international repute and members of concerned non-governmental organizations (NGOs) to discuss common problems, share experiences and seek viable solutions to crime. Their recommendations impact on legislative and policy-making bodies of the United Nations and of national and local governments.

The First Congress   1955

Five hundred and twelve participants met at the Palais des Nations in Geneva, Switzerland, to convene the first UN Crime Congress. Their credentials were strong enough and their backgrounds sufficiently diverse to lend credibility to this fledgling attempt at international cooperation in criminal justice policy. There were delegates from 61 countries and territories, representing 51 Governments; from international organizations such as the International Labour Organisation (ILO), the United Nations Educational, Scientific and Cultural Organization (UNESCO), the World Health Organization (WHO), the Council of Europe and the League of Arab States; and from 43 NGOs. Nearly half were scholars and policymakers, present in their individual capacities.

At this Congress, held in the heart of Western Europe, the nations of Europe fielded the greatest number of governmental delegations (in 1955, half the world's territories were not yet independent and were not represented at the United Nations). The topics of the First Congress accordingly reflected the pressing concerns of post-war Europe. There was an urgent need to set standards for the treatment of prisoners, whose numbers were swelling due to the turmoil and black markets of the war and post-war years. The poignant and bewildering question of how to respond to juvenile delinquency, which was taking root among young people growing up in rubble-strewn streets, often without fathers, was another focus of attention.

Consideration of the proper functioning of penal institutions led to the drafting and adoption by the Congress and subsequent approval by ECOSOC of the 95 Standard Minimum Rules for the Treatment of Prisoners, an expansion of a less comprehensive bill of rights for persons in legal custody that had been drafted by the IPC. Whatever the extent of their crimes, it was felt, prisoners are entitled to human dignity and minimal standards of well-being. This conviction was especially strong among the many delegates present who, during the Second-World-War occupation of countries by Fascist powers, experienced brutality and deprivation while incarcerated. The carefully thought out, comprehensive provisions of the Standard Minimum Rules and the broad representation of national and professional viewpoints incorporated in them exerted a strong moral suasion that over the years has brought improvements to prisons around the world. Its provisions frequently are cited by prisoners protesting substandard conditions.The success of the Standard Minimum Rules paved the way for many other international models, standards, norms and guidelines touching on every aspect of criminal justice and set a precedent for United Nations initiatives to humanize the administration of criminal justice by principles agreed upon by the world community.

Other matters relating to the operation of penal institutions considered by the First Congress included recommendations for the selection, training and status of prison personnel; possibilities for "open" penal and correctional institutions; and appropriate use of prison labour.

Discussion of the prevention of juvenile delinquency attracted the greatest number of participants at the First Congress. Juvenile delinquency was treated as a broad category under which problems relating to youthful offenders as well as abandoned, orphaned and maladjusted minors were dealt with. Prevention was deemed to be the operative concept, and the problem was analyzed in terms of its social, economic and psychological causes.

The Second Congress   1960

At the invitation of the Government of the United Kingdom of Great Britain and Northern Ireland, the Second Congress was convened in London. Selection of this venue initiated the practice of holding the Congresses away from United Nations Headquarters facilities so as to bring them to a wider variety of the world's urban centres. Increased participation reflected the addition of newly independent nations as Member States. Representatives of 70 Governments were in attendance, along with delegates from 50 NGOs and, in addition to the international bodies involved in the First Congress, the Commission for Technical Assistance in Africa South of the Sahara. All in all, there were 1,131 participants, 632 of whom attended as individuals. The large percentage of attendees representing NGOs or chosen because of their scholarly credentials reflected the prevailing view that scientific and social analyses were required to come to grips with the complex problems at hand.

Once again, juvenile delinquency was on the agenda. Under study were newly emerging forms of delinquency, their origin, prevention and treatment; the possibilities of special police forces for the prevention of youthful offences; and the impact of the mass media on the problem. Debate posed supporters of broad treatment programmes for all manner of youthful maladjustments against those who perceived a distinction between the maladjusted and young people who commit crimes for more straightforward reasons. Proponents of the latter view argued that not all delinquents are socially deprived; moreover, no one, juvenile or adult, is perfectly adjusted in every respect. The outcome of the debate was a recommendation that the concept of juvenile delinquency should be restricted to violations of criminal law, excluding vaguely anti-social postures or rebellious attitudes which are widely associated with the process of growing up.

The addition of new Member States to the United Nations required broadening of the largely European perspective of the First Congress. This led to a precedent-setting analysis of crime and criminal justice in relation to overall national development. Two general reports were submitted to the Second Congress on the "Prevention of Types of Criminality Resulting from Social Changes and Accompanying Economic Developments in Less Developed Countries". These examined the relation between socio-economic development and crime prevention in light of available data on demography, the environment, economics, culture, town planning, industrialization and migration. It was recommended that rational planning and social policy-making should be applied to the problem of crime. It was asserted that social breakdown generally precedes the creation of new social codes and values, and that orderly social change is not easily achieved.

Precipitous changes in economic and cultural conditions, the delegates realized, are found in long-established as well as newly independent nations. Discussion of the relation between development and crime therefore was extended to conditions in the developed countries as well. Economic improvement, experts warned, is not a one-way street leading away from crime. Tumultuous, unevenly shared economic growth can also provoke criminal activity

The Third Congress   1965

The Third Congress, convened in Stockholm, Sweden, addressed the ambitious theme of "Prevention of Criminality". The work of the Congress was propelled to a large extent by the enthusiasm of the Swedish hosts, who had embarked on a comprehensive national experiment in crime prevention. Topics on the agenda included a continuation of the discussion on social change and criminality; social forces and the prevention of crime; community-based preventive action; measures to curtail recidivism; probation policies; and special preventive and treatment programmes for young adults, who constitute the most crime-prone sector of the population.

Under the headings of "social change" and "social forces", the effects of urbanization, public opinion, education and migration were dealt with. There was also a specific recommendation to improve the value of studies of criminality through more meticulous official records on offenders.

Seventy-four Governments, 39 NGOs and all of the specialized agencies attending the previous Congress were present in Stockholm. The total number of participants reached 1,083, of whom 658 represented non-governmental bodies. The presence of representatives from a still-increasing pool of newly independent countries bolstered the assertion that developing nations should not restrict themselves to mechanically copying criminal justice institutions developed in Western countries. The hope was expressed that the developing nations would be able to head off by dynamic action in the mental health field many of the phenomena of mental disorders that beset the more developed parts of the world.

The Fourth Congress   1970

Set in the city of Kyoto, once the capital of ancient Japan, this was the first Congress held outside of Europe. The number of participants declined slightly, but the number of Governments represented jumped to 85.

The Fourth Congress convened under the slogan "Crime and Development". Its conclusions centred around the need for crime control and prevention measures — referred to as "social defence policies" — to be built into the development planning of nations. The groundwork for much of the discussion had been laid by a set of working papers prepared by the Secretariat and the World Health Organization and by reports of an ad hoc group of experts. These emphasized the need for social planning to promote economic growth and higher living standards while curtailing crime and delinquency that might result from the disintegration of traditional modes of life. It was emphasized, however, that the promotion of social and economic integration should not be seen as a solution to criminality; it might give rise to the misleading impression that crime control involved little more than provision of social services.

A theme touched on by the Third Congress — community-based prevention — was expanded upon at the Fourth. The positive contributions of public participation to crime prevention and control were explored. The utilization of civic involvement is a strategy which the host nation of Japan had applied with remarkable success.

The Congress also investigated the nation-by-nation implementation of the Standard Minimum Rules for the Treatment of Prisoners, relying on results of a questionnaire previously submitted to Member States.

The use of research as a tool of social policy came under scrutiny. A consensus supported the practical conclusion that the primary object of research was the identification not of the causes of crime per se, but of factors that could be applied to planned action.

The broad scope of the Fourth Congress deliberations — incorporating holistic considerations such as "development" and "social defence policy"— led to a re-ordering of the UN's crime prevention programme and the creation in 1977 of the Committee on Crime Prevention and Control (see Chapter III).

The Fifth Congress   1975

The Fifth Congress on the Prevention of Crime and the Treatment of Offenders returned to Geneva, site of the First Congress. The number of nations represented again increased, to 101, and the participation of specialized agencies was augmented by the presence of Interpol, the IPPC and the Organization for Economic Co-operation and Development (OECD).

The theme of the Fifth Congress was "Crime Prevention and Control: the Challenge of the Last Quarter of the Century". Under this forward-looking rubric, the Congress treated a larger number of specific concerns than ever before. They included:

- Changes in the form and dimensions of criminality, at national and transnational levels;
- Crime as a business and organized crime;
- The role of criminal legislation, judicial procedures and other forms of social control in the prevention of crime;
- The addition of crime-prevention activities and related social services to traditional law enforcement roles of police and other law enforcement agencies;
- Treatment of offenders in custody or in the community, with special reference to implementation of the Standard Minimum Rules;
- Economic and social consequences of crime (including the cost of crime) and new challenges for research and planning;
- Alcohol and drug abuse; and
- Victim compensation as a substitute for retributive criminal justice.

The Fifth Congress was responsible for two notable documents, which stand alongside the Standard Minimum Rules for the Treatment of Offenders as influential international guidelines to criminal justice practice. One was a "Declaration on the Protection of All Persons from Being Subjected to Torture and Other Cruel, Inhuman or Degrading Treatment or Punishment". The Declaration was adopted by General Assembly resolution 3452 (XXX) of 9 December 1975, and led to a subsequent convention on that topic. The Congress also paved the way for drafting the "Code of Conduct for Law Enforcement Officials". The Code, which has been called a Hippocratic oath for police professionals, was adopted by the General Assembly in 1979.

General conclusions reached by the Fifth Congress focussed on the crucial role of social justice in preventing crime, the importance of coordinating criminal justice programmes within overall national social policy and the importance of respect for human rights.

The Sixth Congress   1980

The UN Crime Congress in Caracas, Venezuela, was the first to be hosted by a developing nation and the first to take place in the Western hemisphere. The widespread interest it evoked among long-established and newly independent nations and national liberation groups was reflected in delegations representing 102 nations, and bodies such as the League of Arab States, the Organization for African Unity (OAU), the Pan-Arab Organization for Social Defence, the Palestine Liberation Organization (PLO), the South West Africa People's Organization (SWAPO), the African National Congress (ANC) and the Pan Africanist Congress of Azania.

The theme of the Sixth Congress, "Crime Prevention and the Quality of Life", was elaborated in the first operative paragraph of its Caracas Declaration: ". . . the success of criminal justice systems and strategies for crime prevention, especially in light of the growth of new and sophisticated forms of crime and the difficulties encountered in the administration of criminal justice, depends above all on the progress achieved throughout the world in improving social conditions and enhancing the quality of life . . . ."

Conceptualization of juvenile delinquency, which to some extent had been narrowed by the Second Congress, was once again broadened. Emphasis was placed not only on the application of criminal sanctions to youthful offenders but also on the provision of social justice for all children, so they would not be driven to offend. The Caracas Declaration addressed the need for standard minimum rules for juvenile justice and further research into the causes of juvenile delinquency.

The items relating to juvenile delinquency were among 19 resolutions and 5 decisions involving more than 100 requests for action incorporated in the Caracas Declaration. Among the recommendations were: promotion of broader public participation in crime prevention; improvement of statistics relating to crime and criminals; and eradication of the practice of extra-legal executions, deemed a particularly abhorrent crime and abuse of power.

Contributing to the achievements of the 1980 Congress was the "Report of the Working Group of Experts from Latin America and the Caribbean on Criminal Policy and Development". This expert group promoted the inclusion of criminal justice experts on national development planning boards and the establishment in each Member State of a body responsible for ensuring international cooperation. They also came up with an innovative approach to the question of deciding which actions should be classified as crimes. The Working Group argued that the relationship between development and crime favours a two-way process of criminalization and decriminalization of offences. Thus, the scope of criminal law statutes should be broadened to include wilful actions harmful to the national wealth and well-being — offences such as destruction of the ecology and participation in networks for drug trafficking and trafficking in persons. As a corollary, the Working Group recommended a reduction in the number of statutes covering petty crimes and those of little or no socially destructive effect.

The Seventh Congress 1985

This Congress is best known for the Milan Plan of Action, which called for a concerted response from the community of nations to address socio-economic factors relevant to the commission of crimes. Taking place in the Italian city for which the Plan of Action is named, the Congress dedicated itself to the theme of "Crime Prevention for Freedom, Justice, Peace and Development".

The expanding purview of United Nations criminal justice concerns presented the delegates with an imposing agenda: 21 major substantive documents deriving from General Assembly and ECOSOC mandates were prepared for the Congress, in addition to previously issued reports of regional and interregional preparatory meeting.

The work of the Congress was organized under five topic headings.

- "New Dimensions of Criminality and Crime Prevention in the Context of Development" continued and updated UN interest in the relation between social development policies and criminal justice systems. Fraud and crime in international commerce and financial transfers was one of the areas under scrutiny.

- "Criminal Justice Processes and Perspectives in a Changing World" covered the need to revise, reform or reinforce the workings of criminal justice systems.

- "Victims of Crime" addressed the rights of victims of crime and abuse of power, compensation and restitution schemes and means of assisting them through criminal justice systems.
- "Youth, Crime and Justice" extended perennial UN interest in members of the age bracket with the highest percentage of criminal offenders.
- "Formulation and Application of United Nations Standards and Norms in Criminal Justice" constituted a review of the value of UN instruments in the criminal justice field and the extent of their implementation among Member States.

In addition to the Milan Plan of Action, five other major international instruments setting norms and standards were approved by consensus:

- Guiding Principles for Crime Prevention and Criminal Justice in the Context of Development;
- United Nations Standard Minimum Rules for the Administration of Juvenile Justice;
- Declaration of Basic Principles of Justice for Victims of Crime and Abuse of Power;
- Basic Principles on the Independence of the Judiciary;
- Model Agreement on the Transfer of Foreign Prisoners and Recommendations on the Treatment of Foreign Prisoners.

The Eighth Congress   1990

The United Nations Crime Congress returned to Latin America in 1990. The Eighth Congress was convened in the Palacio de Convenciones in Havana, Cuba, under the theme of "International Crime Prevention and Criminal Justice in the Twenty-First Century".

The Eighth Congress maintained the UN's traditional portfolio of concerns while dealing with contemporary developments. Among the latter were a growing alertness to the theft of archaeological treasures, the dumping of hazardous wastes in ocean waters, the flourishing international trade in illicit drugs and the lethal connection between drug abuse and AIDS and the appearance of both among prison populations.

Offering encouragement for the future were the lessening of tensions between the Eastern and Western blocs of nations, increased awareness of the value of international cooperation in the law enforcement field, and presentations and exchanges of experience regarding new techniques such as computer networks and provisions for seizing the financial proceeds of organized crime and examining bank records.

Despite the growing body of information and experience relating criminal justice planning with socio-economic development, it was recognized that the international debt crisis, steep declines in primary commodity prices and general outflow of capital from the many of the developing countries pose a threat to progress in this area.

Reflecting these hopes and concerns, the Eighth Congress produced more international instruments than all the preceding Congresses put together. Five model treaties recommended to and later approved by the General Assembly covered bilateral agreements on extradition, mutual assistance in criminal investigations and other matters, transfer of proceedings in criminal prosecutions, transfer of supervision of offenders and prevention of crimes infringing on the cultural heritage of peoples. Six major documents were adopted setting guidelines on criminal justice system standards, ranging from non-custodial measures to the prevention of juvenile delinquency.

Resolutions drawn up in Havana dealt with, *inter alia*, the computerization of criminal justice operations, the problem of domestic violence, the instrumental use of children in criminal activities, the role of criminal law in protecting nature and the environment, computer-related crime, corruption in government and measures to prevent infection of prisoners with HIV/AIDS.

In a resolution detailing measures against international terrorism, the Congress urged States to consider favourably national and international action against terrorism. An annex to the resolution lists a number of areas of particular concern. Among these are State policies and practices that may be considered a violation of international treaty obligations; the absence of specific norms on State responsibility for carrying out international obligations; abuse of diplomatic immunity; lack of international regulation of the trade in arms; and the inadequacy of international mechanisms for peaceful resolution of conflicts and enforcement of human rights. The annex calls for greater uniformity in laws concerning territorial and extraterritorial jurisdiction and bilateral and multilateral cooperation between police, prosecutors and the judiciaries of Member States. It also recommends looking into the possibility of an international criminal court or some other international mechanism with jurisdiction over offences including those connected with terrorism and illicit trafficking in narcotic drugs or psychotropic substances.

Another task of the Congress was to review the UN's criminal justice programme. On the recommendation of the Eighth Congress, the General Assembly subsequently adopted a resolution convening a Ministerial Meeting on the Creation of an Effective United Nations Crime Prevention and Criminal Justice Programme, which in turn led to the establishment in 1992 of the UN Commission of Crime Prevention and Criminal Justice (see Chapter III).

The Ninth Congress 1995

New measures for combating international crime syndicates, terrorism, ecological crimes, violence inflicted on women, illegal traffic in aliens and corruption of public officials were recommended by the Congress held in Cairo, Egypt.

"Crime in its various dimensions and forms is a problem requiring coordinated international action, with close cooperation among States", Secretary-General Boutros Boutros-Ghali said in a message delivered to the Congress, held in his native country.

Emphasizing that the UN regards crime as a crucial development issue, the Secretary-General said that "economies in crisis, or in a delicate period of transition, need help from the international community to combat the dangers posed by crime".

The first UN Crime Congress on the African continent and the first to take place in the Arab world was attended by 1,732 participants from 138 countries and 15 intergovernmental and 48 non-governmental organizations, as well as 22 United Nations agencies and programmes. Among the 1,290 governmental representatives were 33 Ministers of Justice and 6 Ministers of the Interior, along with heads of police agencies, public prosecutors, high-ranking judges and heads of prison systems.

Endorsement by the Congress of a wide array of measures to combat transnational crime reflected the growth of consensus among Governments and experts that international cooperation is needed if the rapid spread of criminal syndicates is to be stemmed.

An early focus of the Congress was on a draft resolution calling attention to links between terrorism and organized crime and calling for concerted international action to combat both. Several delegations and experts pointed out that condemning both kinds of organizations should not be taken to mean that terrorist organizations are simply an adjunct to crime syndicates. Such an identification might lead to injustices against organizations or popular causes incorrectly labelled as "terrorist". The final resolution adopted by the Congress condemned terrorist acts and recommended to the Commission that it examine further links between these acts and organized transnational crime.

In another action, the Congress asked that the views of States be solicited on the possible elaboration of new international instruments — such as a convention — against organized transnational crime. Such a treaty, the resolution suggested, might cover arrangements for international cooperation at the investigative, prosecutorial and judicial levels and for prevention and control of money laundering. A similar measure was adopted at the World Ministerial Conference on Transnational Crime, held in Naples, Italy in 1994 (see Chapter I).

An omnibus resolution asked States to facilitate transnational criminal investigations through extradition, provision of relevant records, exchange of evidence, and cooperation in locating persons, serving subpoenas and carrying out inspections and seizures. It also called for stricter laws on registration of imported motor vehicles, as a means to combat the large-scale trafficking in stolen cars.

In response to widespread concern about the involvement of organized crime in smuggling and selling weapons, a resolution was adopted calling for urgent measures to restrict international traffic in firearms and urging States to regulate more closely domestic availability.

A strongly worded resolution urged States to adopt laws against acts of violence that may victimize women and sanctions against rape, domestic violence, sexual abuse and all practices harmful to females, including the traditional practice in some societies of genital mutilation. Legal measures prohibiting harassment, intimidation or threats against women or their families, and laws regulating the acquisition and storage of firearms in the home are also recommended by the same resolution of the Congress. States are asked to take special account of women's vulnerability toviolence — including murder, torture, systematic rape and sexual slavery — in situations of armed conflict.

Plenary discussions and a wide variety of workshops presenting groundbreaking research projects led to wide-ranging debate and discussion, including the following:

- An unprecedented debate on corruption of public officials was introduced by an international panel of five experts. They noted the increasing interaction between cases of official corruption and transnational crime organizations. It was stated that corruption affects all countries, although it is often rooted in entrepreneurial opportunism of businesses in the industrialized countries. Many of the recommendations made during the debate involving Congress participants as well as the panelists were later taken by the Commission, which at its fourth session recommended to ECOSOC the adoption of a resolution on the subject (ECOSOC 1995.14, of 24 July 1995).

- A Congress workshop discussed both the bene
fits and the potential problems of using criminal
justice systems to protect the environment.
Forms of ecological crime mentioned included
the illegal disposal and trafficking of hazardous
wastes, smuggling or theft of cultural treasures,
and newer forms such as the illicit release of
genetically engineered organisms into natural
environments. Proposals ranged from elaborating
a detailed list of environmental crimes and
establishing special police and prosecution units
to an international convention on the protection
of the environment. Establishment of a world
environmental protection agency under UN
auspices was also suggested.

- Another innovative workshop investigated the
role of the mass media in crime prevention.
Dramatic testimony by journalists from Russia,
Kenya, India, the Philippines and the United
States underscored the importance of the media's
watchdog function and its potential in preventing crime. Participants recommended that the
United Nations reassert the "enormous importance of a free press as part of the democratic
process" and commit resources for countering
the negative effects of the mass media on young
people; call upon Governments to create an
education campaign to ensure that crimes against
the environment are recognized in the media as
criminal and moral offences; and encourage,
through the media, the development of ways to
eradicate violence against women, enhancing
respect for their dignity and discouraging
negative stereotyping.

- An urban policy workshop analysed successful
prevention policies, including grass-roots participation in criminal justice systems, appropriate
design of housing complexes and public spaces,
consultations among government agencies
and between the public and the private sectors,
and the strengthening of social safety nets.
While highlighting workable solutions to crime,
participants cautioned against ignoring the
growing feeling of urban insecurity. Unveiled at
the workshop was a global "victimization survey"
conducted by the Rome-based UN Interregional
Crime and Justice Research Institute
(see Chapter VI).

In addition to workshops, a variety of ancillary meetings were organized by NGOs. One of them, conducted by the International Scientific and Professional Advisory Council of the UN crime prevention and criminal justice programme, produced a comprehensive investigation of the relation between crime and migration. Speakers detailed the involvement of transnational crime syndicates in trafficking in illegal aliens and identified factors that tend to make legal and illegal migrants both victims and perpetrators of crime. A report written for the Congress advocated reducing motivations for emigration, concluding that "the problem of migration cannot be solved satisfactorily at the border . . . [it] has to be solved at the frontiers of a cleaner environment, more economic development and good government".

Chapter 5

Technical Cooperation and Advisory Services

Direct services to Governments in the form of advisory services for policy formulation and implementation and training of personnel have been a distinctive aspect of crime prevention and control work since the earliest days of the Organization. A system of advisory services was in place by 1946, antedating much larger and better-known programmes of technical assistance in economic development.

In the years immediately following, the most economically developed, industrialized countries were those that commonly made use of United Nations advisory services. Practically all of the highly developed nations chose senior officials to travel abroad, under United Nations auspices and financing, to observe and consult on practice and policy in other industrialized nations, particularly those with reputations for innovative or progressive programmes. As the composition of the United Nations shifted numerically and geographically, and as its commitment to the needs of the developing world intensified, it became customary to concentrate on the needs of the less affluent countries.

Not only the range of countries receiving assistance but also the scope of the programmes themselves has broadened over the years. Requests for expertise early on tended to focus on highly specific areas, such as the introduction of juvenile courts, open penal institutions, new forms of probation and so on. Now there is greater interest in examining the totality of Governments' efforts in coping with crime, and growing recognition that crime and society's approach to it are intimately bound to the socio-economic fabric of a country.

Two major objectives can be served through technical assistance and advisory services: strengthening the criminal justice systems of Governments, often overwhelmed by outbreaks of crime and a multiplicity of development imperatives, and advancing new policies. Under real-life circumstances, theory and practice tend to go hand in hand. The training of personnel leads to an analysis of current practice and how it may be improved, while the formulation of innovative policy requires the training of officials from senior levels down to clerical, custodial, police and administrative staff in new modes of practice.

Advisory services exchange programmes between criminal justice personnel and experts of different countries serve a third purpose: the development of a worldwide perspective. This is of particular importance in regard to implementing United Nations stan-

dards, guidelines, international instruments and other policy recommendations. A frequent complaint among States that have
endorsed such resolutions is the difficulty of practical implementation. Governments with strained budgets and a multiplicity of pressing political, economic and social needs are hard pressed to upgrade
standards of criminal justice practice and install new approaches.
Technical and advisory assistance is needed to move ahead on either
front.

International Cooperation

The United Nations also operates under budgetary constraints, and
demand for advisory and technical services invariably outstrips the
capacities of the Organization. One means of breaking this impasse
is increased support from Governments and non-governmental
organizations, in the form of cash contributions, in-kind donations,
expert services, fellowships or other kinds of assistance. A number of
technical assistance and advisory projects accordingly are being formulated with a view to obtaining support from donor countries, the
Department for Development Support and Management Services of
the Secretariat, the United Nations Development Programme, the
World Bank and other internationally oriented agencies.

A source of technical support at the national and region-
al levels that has not reached its full potential is the United Nations
Crime Prevention and Criminal Justice Fund. To date, the number of
Governments contributing to the Fund does not exceed 7 per cent
of the membership of the United Nations. Recognizing that the
Fund could be an invaluable international resource, the Crime
Congresses as well as the General Assembly have repeatedly invited
Governments to make financial contributions.

Ongoing international cooperation is frequently a by-
product of United Nations assistance programmes. Many experts
sent on assignments by the United Nations are on leave from high
government posts, granted by their Governments for that purpose.
Upon return, experts frequently spark within their own Govern-
nments a special interest in follow-up to their work, through the
provision of fellowships for further training or the provision of
equipment or training materials. Assistance between countries and
the interchange of criminal justice personnel have also been moti-
vated by the activities of the regional and interregional institutes of
the United Nations and the spirit of intra-national cooperation that
arises from seminars with participants from many nations.

The Work of the Crime Prevention and Criminal Justice Division

Among its functions and capabilities (see Chapter III), the United Nations Crime Prevention and Criminal Justice Division is the central repository of international technical expertise in matters of crime prevention and criminal justice, criminal law reform and criminological sciences. Located at the United Nations Office at Vienna, the Division bears a primary responsibility within the United Nations system for facilitating and delivering technical cooperation in the criminal justice field and providing technical and advisory services.

Assistance to Governments may take many forms. Fellowships allow criminal justice professionals the chance to study techniques in another country and bring knowledge of new or different approaches and the practical dimensions of their execution back to their home nations. Conversely, experts dispatched to a requesting country are able to confer with senior officials, institute training programmes, assist in the analysis of local criminal justice policy or otherwise impart techniques and approaches of proven validity.

Many assistance projects have entailed the provision of expertise on a relatively long-term basis, generally up to one or two years. In 1970, the position of Interregional Adviser was established within the Crime Prevention and Criminal Justice Branch to provide quicker, more flexible services. Within the first four years, the Interregional Adviser responded to requests — largely for evaluation, research and planning — from 40 countries. Between 1982 and 1994, the number of requests mushroomed to more than 200. The position of a second Interregional Adviser was established in 1994.

Services available to the world community

A broad repertoire of services for Member States and regional bodies is available from the Division. Advisory Missions of two to three weeks' duration are run by the Interregional Advisers, helping to implement United Nations standards and guidelines and to plan national programmes. There are also Project Formulation Missions, dealing with specific crime prevention or crime control policy areas and the organization of suitable training programmes.

The Division, in cooperation with donor countries and agencies, may install resident advisers and trainers and assist with the procurement of equipment such as computers, forensic apparatus and training materials.

Large projects must be financed by donor countries, financial institutions or the United Nations Development Programme. Funds for innovative demonstration projects and for ad hoc advisory services on occasion may be obtained from the United Nations Regular Programme Budget. The Division also cooperates with donor agencies and private institutions and can help formulate multilateral projects of cooperation suited to recipient country needs.

Assistance is provided in the following technical areas:

Criminal law and procedure

- Codification and digests of existing legislation and jurisprudence

- Penal law reform

- Decriminalization and depenalization policies

- Classification of crimes and model codes

- Commercial crime, fraud and tax evasion

- Corruption, embezzlement and misconduct in office

- Organized crime, racketeering and smuggling

- Offences against public safety, cultural patrimony and the environment

- Criminal law procedures and the rights of the accused

- Alternatives to imprisonment

- Extradition and the treatment of foreign prisoners

- Bilateral treaties in criminal matters

Criminal justice management

- System analysis and organizations and structure of justice agencies

- Computerization and management systems

- Allocation of manpower, training, and human resource development

- Research on interrelationships between socio-economic factors and crime

- Incorporation of crime prevention strategies in national, regional and urban development

- Status, selection and training of criminal justice personnel, including judges and prosecutors

- Improving the efficacy and fairness of judicial processes

- Facilitating access to justice and legal assistance for the poor

- Role of lawyers and public defenders

Criminal justice statistics

- Organization of data collection and record-keeping

- Computerization

- Crime trends and surveys; crime forecasting

- Manpower statistics and budget allocations

- Criminal records and management

- Judicial statistics and assignment of cases

- Prison population statistics

- Recidivism statistics

Law enforcement

- Code of conduct

- Use of force and firearms by law enforcement officials

- Community support, role of the mass media and complaint procedures

- Policies re: victims of crime and domestic violence

- Investigative techniques re: money-laundering and organized crime

- International cooperation to combat transnational offenders

- Seizure of assets derived from illegal activities

- Forensic training and the handling and transfer of evidence

- Arrest procedures and the protection of human rights

Rehabilitation of offenders

- Alternatives to imprisonment: community-based programmes, halfway houses and electronic monitoring

- Probation, supervision programmes and after-care services

- Programmes in correctional institutions: weekend imprisonment, semi-liberty, training programmes and supervised labour

- Prisoners' rights and privileges, furloughs and ombudsmen

- Treatment of women in prisons

- Treatment of drug addicts in prisons

- Treatment of mentally ill offenders

- Treatment of prisoners with AIDS

- Evaluation of correctional programmes and recidivism

- Long-term prisoners and ageing prison populations

Victims of crime

- Policies and procedures designed to protect victims and model laws in this regard

- Restitution and compensation programmes and financing schemes

- Health, social and legal services for victims: child protection, shelters for battered women, rape crisis center

- Victim involvement in judicial proceedings; alternatives to judicial process

- Special police services and procedures for victims and relevant training programmes

- Reporting of victimization and victim studies

- Compensation for victims of abuse of public and economic power

Juvenile justice

- Age of criminal responsibility

- Diversion and non-institutional treatment

- Delinquency prevention strategies

- Mobilization of volunteers and other community services

- Guiding principles in adjudication and disposition

- Institutional treatment—minimum standards

- Multi-sectoral, multi-agency rehabilitation programmes

- Research and planning for policy formulation

- Training of juvenile justice personnel.

Further information may be obtained from:

United Nations Crime Prevention and
Criminal Justice Division
United Nations Office at Vienna
Room E1233
P.O. Box 500
A-1400 Vienna, Austria
Tel.: 43-1-21-345-4269
Fax: 43-1-21-345-5898
Cable address: UNATIONS VIENNA
Telex: 135612
E-mail: aboulouk@unov.or.at

Chapter 6
Affiliated and Associated Institutes

From the beginning, United Nations criminal justice policy has been formulated with a worldwide perspective. Already by the 1950s, however, there was also recognition of the need for regional centres to serve groups of countries that share similar traditions and experience closely related crime problems.

Accordingly, when regional seminars for preparation of the First Crime Congress were held, it was suggested at the meetings taking place in 1953 at Rio de Janeiro and São Paulo, Brazil, that a Latin American institute be established. Among its main purposes would be organizing training courses, conducting research in the field of criminal justice, assisting Governments of the region, providing advisory opinions on policy matters, organizing regional seminars and facilitating cooperation among the States of the region and with the United Nations. Similar proposals came from the Arab seminar at Cairo, Egypt, in 1953 and the Asia and Far East seminar at Rangoon, Burma (now Myanmar), in 1954.

At present, regional institutes affiliated with the United Nations serve Asia and the Pacific region, Latin America, Europe and Africa, and an interregional institute is situated in Rome. There are also UN-associated institutes serving the Arab States, North America and Oceania.

UNICRI

United Nations Interregional Crime and Justice Research Institute

Established in 1968 as the United Nations Social Defence Research Institute (UNSDRI), the Institute was originally conceived as the research arm of the United Nations criminal justice programme. As the Institute's work expanded, research was increasingly applied to training and field activities on behalf of developing countries In May 1989 ECOSOC adopted a new Statute, transforming UNSDRI into UNICRI and updating the Institute's terms of reference and *modus operandi* to incorporate this broadened and result-oriented approach.

Activities of the United Nations institute may be loosely grouped under five categories: action-oriented research (pride of place being given to an international comparative approach at the interregional level and, secondarily, the regional level); technical cooperation; training; library and documentation services; and publications. UNICRI's current work includes projects on:

- Crime and development
- Sentencing policy and practice, with emphasis on alternatives to imprisonment
- Crime prevention and social control
- Environmental crime
- Juvenile delinquency and juvenile justice
- Drug abuse prevention and control
- Economic crime
- Training courses in research methodology
- Training courses for judicial personnel and social operators.

UNICRI maintains close consultative and cooperative relationships with the Crime Prevention and Criminal Justice Division and also works closely with the regional institutes and with relevant United Nations programmes and agencies. The Institute organizes the research components of the United Nations Crime Congresses and, in collaboration with the Division, prepares documentation for each upcoming Congress.

The Institute library holds more than 15,000 monographs, and approximately 500 serial titles (printed and CD-ROM). Of particular importance is the collection of documents, mainly from the United Nations and the Council of Europe, as well as pamphlets and grey literature. Acquisition policy is based on an interdisciplinary approach: while texts on penal law and criminology comprise the core of the collection, there are also social science methodology reports on socio-economic conditions and on social policy interventions.

UNICRI is assuming a leading role in the development of the United Nations Criminal Justice Information Programme and in analysing and disseminating the results of the United Nations Crime Surveys. *Its International Crime (Victim) Survey,* prepared in time for the Ninth Crime Congress, is the most comprehensive effort to date to assess the incidence of crime worldwide through personal interviews with samples drawn from the general population. Also designed to aid the Ninth Congress was a study of criminal justice responses to attacks on natural environments, based on 90 case studies of 11 countries on six continents (see Chapter IV). Since 1974, UNICRI has published six editions of its *World Directory of Criminological Institutes.*

UNICRI's headquarters are situated in the historic centre of Rome, occupying a seventeenth-century building originally erected as a progressive custodial facility dedicated by Pope Innocent X to "justice and clemency" and "the more secure and better custody of criminals". The facility is placed at UNICRI's disposal by the Government of Italy.

United Nations Interregional Crime and
Justice Research Institute
Via Giulia, 52-00186
Rome, Italy
Tel.: 39-6-687-7437
Fax: 39-6-689-2638
Telex: 610181 Fao I Unicri
E-mail: unicri.org@agora.stm.it
Cable: UNICRI 00186 Roma

UNAFEI

Asia and Far East Institute for the Prevention of Crime and the Treatment of offenders

The first of the United Nations criminological institutes, UNAFEI carries out an extensive programme of training, technical cooperation, research, documentation and publications from a modern facility in Fuchu, on the outskirts of Tokyo, Japan.

Since its establishment in 1962 and through 1995, UNAFEI conducted 101 international seminars and training courses for professionals with ranking positions in police forces, prosecutors' offices, the judiciary, correctional services and probationary and welfare agencies. Three-month training courses are held twice a year, and there is an annual month-long seminar to meet the needs of top-level administrators and policymakers.

In addition, UNAFEI conducts overseas joint seminars in cooperation with host Governments to discuss how to improve criminal justice administrations and combat organized crime and drug trafficking. UNAFEI staff are dispatched to nations in Asia and the Pacific region to arrange two-week seminars, attended by high-ranking policymakers, administrators and academicians. Through 1995, UNAFEI has conducted 16 of these joint seminars, in Sri Lanka, Malaysia, the Philippines, Papua New Guinea, Indonesia, Thailand, China, Singapore, Nepal, the Republic of Korea and Pakistan. The discussions also served to to update participants on new United Nations criminal justice policies, services and publications.

To enhance the ability of criminal justice personnel to cope with drug offences, UNAFEI and the Japan International Cooperation Agency (JICA) have conducted regional professional seminars in Costa Rica since 1987, and in Thailand since 1992.

Past technical cooperation projects include a comparative survey of juvenile delinquency in Asia and the Far East, research on open correctional institutions in the same region, and work on implementing the standard minimum rules for the treatment of prisoners in Asia.

UNAFEI also holds workshops on criminal justice issues in cooperation with other UN agencies.

Visiting experts and participants in the training courses contribute articles to a frequently published "Resource Material Series", and the Institute summarizes the results of each training session in its *UNAFEI Newsletter*. Among the books available free of charge are *Drug Control in Asia, Crime and Justice in Asia and the Pacific*, and *An Empirical Study on Development and Crime Prevention*. Recent UNAFEI publications include *Asia Crime Report No.1, Crime Trends in Asia and the Pacific* and *Criminal Justice Profiles of Asia*.

The Institute's Fuchu facility includes a dormitory, a conference hall, a library, an auditorium, seminar rooms and Japanese-style guest rooms for students and visiting lecturers.

For the first five years of UNAFEI's existence, administrative responsibility was borne equally by the United Nations and the Government of Japan. Financial assistance from the United Nations began to decline in 1966, and was discontinued in 1970. Since that time, virtually all administrative and financial obligations have been assumed by the Government of Japan. The Director of UNAFEI is appointed in consultation with the United Nations.

Asia and Far East Institute for the Prevention of
Crime and the Treatment of Offenders
1-26, Harumi-cho
Fuchu
Tokyo, Japan 183
Tel.: 81-423-33-7021
Fax: 81-423-33-7024, -68-8500
E-mail: ldj00272@niftyserve.or.jp

ILANUD

The United Nations Latin American Institute for the Prevention of Crime and the Treatment of Delinquency

ILANUD was founded in 1975 under the terms of an agreement between the United Nations and the Government of Costa Rica, with the mission of encouraging and supporting the countries of Latin America and the Caribbean in strengthening their criminal justice systems, preventing crime and restructuring mechanisms of social control.

ILANUD's approach to attaining these objectives is to assist the United Nations in five action areas: citizen security, environmental crimes and misdemeanors, public corruption, new forms of organized crime and management of justice systems. These fields of action were chosen on the basis of relevant UN guidelines, the expressed needs of countries, the Institute's specialities and strengths, and optimal international cooperation. ILANUD addresses these issues through implementation of programmes and projects entailing research, technical assistance, training and dissemination of scientific information.

One of the Institute's most important activities in this regard is development of the Administration of Justice Information System for Latin America (AJIS), which provides information services to justice-sector institutions, academic centres, organizations affiliated with the justice sector and international cooperation agencies. The AJIS consists of eight databases: international cooperation agencies, studies and assessments, experts, legislation, agenda, crime policies, statistics and international documents.

The United Nations Latin American Institute for
Crime Prevention and the Treatment of Offenders
P.O. Box 10071-1000
San José, Costa Rica
Tel.: 506-257-5826
Fax: 506-233-7175
E-mail: ilanud@sol.racsa.com.c.r

The United Nations African Regional Institute for the Prevention of Crime and the Treatment of Offenders

UNAFRI

Since 1989, UNAFRI has concentrated on providing training and human resources development, policy advice and information and documentation for criminal justice systems on the African continent.

A pilot survey on "African Crime, Criminal Justice Administration and Victimization" was completed in May 1993. That same year workshops were held on the subjects of penal law reform, training for administrators and implementation of United Nations standards and guidelines. In 1994, a Joint Meeting of African Ministers of Justice and Internal Affairs was held at the Institute's headquarters in Kampala, Uganda, in conjunction with a regional meeting in preparation for the Ninth Crime Congress.

Through 1995, 13 seminar reports have been published and distributed and a UNAFRI newsletter has been published twice yearly, work was also initiated on an African crime data bank.

The work of UNAFRI has been interrupted by a recent financial crisis, and arrangements to secure consistent funding are under way.

UNAFRI Secretariat
P.O. Box 10590
Kampala, Uganda
Tel.: 256-41-285-236
Fax: 256-41-221-119

The European Institute for Crime Prevention and Control

HEUNI

Formerly known as the Helsinki Institute, HEUNI was established by a 1981 United Nations agreement with Finland to promote cooperation in crime prevention and control among the countries of Europe with different socio-economic systems. Budgetary responsibility for HEUNI lies with the Government of Finland, although other Governments have also supported the Institute financially.

With the rapid reform of formerly centralized economies in Europe, the Institute has increasingly focused on the needs of emerging democracies in the central and eastern part of the continent. Advice and assistance have been provided in areas such as police standards, drug trafficking, prison administration and domestic violence. HEUNI and the Hungarian Ministry of Justice arranged a seminar on strategies for confronting domestic violence, based on a resource manual which the Institute helped to prepare. In cooperation with the Slovenian authorities, HEUNI furthermore is planning to organize a pilot course for central and eastern Europe on preventing domestice violence. Projects to assist with computerization of criminal justice systems in Bulgaria and Russia are also under way.

European seminars organized by HEUNI are attended by senior government officials and criminological experts from across the continent. The topics are defined and planned by a working group of experts from different countries and fields, a project coordinator prepares documentation for the meetings, and the proceedings of the seminar and report of the project coordinator are published.

Smaller "meetings of experts" explore specific issues in depth. Such meetings at times are convened to offer a European perspective on draft documents of United Nations criminal justice policy.

The topics covered in the European seminars, the meetings of experts and additional research projects are selected in accordance with the criminal justice programme of the United Nations and current priorities within the European region.

Beginning with the first European seminar, on "The Feasibility of a European Information System on Trends in Crime and Criminal Policy", HEUNI has been actively involved with plans for a global United Nations information system on crime and criminal justice. Preparatory work includes ascertaining present and projected needs for various types of information, charting sources such as databanks and experts from European countries and study of the appropriate technology for gathering, processing and disseminating information.

HEUNI has further contributed to the work of the United Nations crime prevention programme by advising on organizational restructuring, preparing reports and papers for Crime Congresses and planning for and analysing the four UN crime surveys.

HEUNI has established a publications series for dissemination of reports of projects, proceedings of the European seminars and contributions from European experts. Among the titles are *The Legal Scope of Non-Prosecution in Europe, The Role of the Victim of Crime in European Criminal Justice Systems, Non-Custodial Alternatives in Europe, Criminal Law and the Environment, Policing in Central and Eastern Europe, Foreigners in Prison, Crime and Criminal Justice in Europe and North America 1986-1990, Directory of Criminal Justice Computer Applications 1995* and *Crime Prevention Strategies in Europe and North America*. HEUNI's *Newsletter* is published twice yearly.

The European Institute for
Crime Prevention and Control
P.O. Box 161
FIN-00131
Helsinki, Finland
Tel.: 358-0-18251
Fax: 358-0-1825-7890
E-mail: heuni@joutsen.pp.fi

The Arab Security Studies and Training Centre

Located in Riyadh, Saudi Arabia, the Centre is an intergovernmental organization, a specialized regional centre servicing the Arab world under the aegis of the Council of Ministers of the Interior of the League of Arab States, as well as an institute associated with the UN's Crime and Criminal Justice Programme.

A six-member board of directors, chaired by the Minister of the Interior of the Kingdom of Saudi Arabia, governs the Centre. All of the Arab League countries are members of the Centre and contribute to its budget.

The Centre's activities are geared to the context of Arab socio-economic and cultural conditions, utilizing a cross-sectoral and interdisciplinary approach. The Centre's work programme emphasizes comparative research and policy development, specialized literature and documentation services, training and graduate education and technical cooperation.

The Centre's components include a research facility, a security information centre, a consultancy office, a specialized library and publishing house, a Graduate School of Criminal Justice, a training institute, a department of symposia and scientific meetings, forensic sciences laboratories, security exhibitions, an international cooperation department and an audio-visual unit.

Since commencing operations in 1981, the Research Centre has carried out 121 research projects and studies. Advanced academic programmes for security personnel and criminal justice professionals are conducted by the Centre's Graduate School of Criminal Justice, covering areas such as Islamic criminal justice, drug control, civil protection and safety, traffic management, criminal investigation, rehabilitation in correctional institutions and police leadership. The Consultative Bureau responds to requests for technical cooperation and advice from Governments, and a computer centre collects and analyses statistics and stays on-line with international databases.

The Centre publishes a number of periodical journals and newsletters, including *The Arab Journal for Security Studies and Training* (bi-annual), a monthly magazine, a monthly newsletter in English, and the newsletter of the International Scientific and Advisory Council of the United Nations, as well as books, reports and other materials.

An expanding array of conferences, symposia, expert meetings, public lectures and public exhibitions are sponsored by the Centre. In recent years, the topics covered include issues such as money laundering, car theft, drug control, tourism security, the role of education in combating crime, and management of correctional institutions.

In January 1988, the Centre hosted a United Nations international conference on research and crime prevention, focusing on alternatives to imprisonment; and an international meeting of experts to help develop the draft United Nations Standards for the Prevention of Juvenile Delinquency was convened at Riyadh in March 1988 at the invitation of the Centre. The Centre also took an active role in preparations for the Ninth Crime Congress, held in Cairo in 1995.

Review of the functioning and work programme of the Arab Security Studies and Training Centre as a regional Arab centre in the fields of crime prevention and criminal justice indicates that it is striving to attain its major objectives: the reduction of criminality, improved efficiency and efficacy of criminal justice administration and the promotion of professional standards of conduct.

> The Arab Security Studies and
> Training Centre
> P.O. Box 6830
> Riyadh 11452, Saudi Arabia
> Tel.: 966-1-246-3444
> Fax: 966-1-246-4713
> Telex: 400949:AMNIYA SJ

AIC   *The Austrialian Institute of Criminology*

The AIC is an Australian federal government agency, established in 1973 to engage in research and related activities in the field of criminology. From the outset, the Institute fulfilled obligations and responsibilities in the international and regional arenas. Its involvement in United Nations activities dates to a Memorandum of Understanding signed with the Crime Prevention and Criminal Justice Division in July 1988.

The Institute advises the Division on implementation of its programme and collaborates in seminars and training courses. It cooperates with UNAFEI in the collection of data and statistics in Asia and the Pacific, takes part in preparations for UN Crime Congresses, hosts international visitors and maintains regional and interregional links with the relevant United Nations bodies. Special emphasis is given to implementation of crime prevention and criminal justice programmes in the countries of the Pacific region, and this has involved the director of the Institute and other staff in delivering lectures, attending conferences and discussing matters of mutual interest with government officials of those countries.

AIC research has specialized in violence against women, aboriginal justice issues, drug issues, environmental crime, fraud control and police administration. Its Deaths in Custody Monitoring Programme was established in 1992, following the investigation of the Royal Commission into Aboriginal deaths in custody; the AIC also maintains a homicide monitoring programme and a crime and violence prevention programme.

The Institute's J.V. Barry Library holds one of the world's foremost criminological collections. Publications include a series on "Trends and Issues in Crime and Criminal Justice", a quarterly journal called *Criminology Australia* and a monograph series on "Australian Studies in Law, Crime and Justice". The AIC catalogue lists approximately 250 backlist titles, available from the publications programme.

Australian Institute of Criminology
G.P.O. Box 2944
Canberra ACT 2601, Australia
Tel.: 61-6-260-9200
Fax: 61-6-260-9201
E-mail: adamg@act.crime.oz.au

The International Centre for Criminal Law Reform and Criminal Justice Policy

The International Centre for Criminal Law Reform and Criminal Justice Policy, founded in 1991 in Vancouver, Canada, as a joint initiative of the University of British Columbia, Simon Fraser University, and the Society for the Reform of Criminal Law, became affiliated with the United Nations in July 1995.

The objective of the Centre is to improve the quality of justice through reform of criminal law, policy and practice. The Centre promotes democratic principles, the rule of law and respect for human rights in criminal law and in the administration of criminal justice — domestically, regionally and globally. It provides advice, information, research and proposals for policy development and legislation. Giving primary emphasis to information and knowledge, the Centre is actively involved in education and training. The Centre also provides technical assistance to Governments and other agencies as appropriate.

The Centre has contributed to and is active in global efforts to create a permanent International Criminal Court of Criminal Jurisdiction. It is also active in research in the areas of combating organized crime, including money-laundering; corruption of public officials; and enforcement and prevention options.

In response to a growing need for renewal of criminal justice institutions, the International Centre has completed a review of activities in the field of sentencing and corrections. A consultation document entitled "Opportunities for Renewal in Sentencing and Corrections" serves as the focal point for this work, which is carried out in cooperation with the Correctional Service of Canada and other national and international partners. The goal in this programmatic area is to put universally recognized human values and principles applicable to sentencing and corrections into practice.

In collaboration with the Division and UNICRI, the Centre is developing a reference document on the role, preparation and performance of civilian peace-keeping police.

The Centre has developed a training curriculum for criminal justice professionals working against domestic violence, and also provided technical assistance in the development of training courses.

The International Centre for Criminal Law
Reform and Criminal Justice Policy at the
University of British Columbia
Legal Annex II, Faculty of Law
1822 East Mall, Vancouver, B.C., Canada V6T 1Z1
Tel.: 604-822-9875
Fax: 604-822-9317
E-mail: prefont@law.ubc.ca

The International Institute of Higher Studies in Criminal Sciences

Also entering the United Nations network of institutes in the 1990s is the International Institute of Higher Studies in Criminal Sciences, located in Siracusa, Italy. Formal association, however, follows a long informal relationship. Founded in 1972, the Siracusa institute is devoted to studies, research and the advancement of criminal sciences, with particular emphasis on human rights.

The Institute prepared a draft convention on the prevention and suppression of torture, which was submitted to the United Nations in 1978 and adopted by the General Assembly as a formal Convention in 1984. Other international instruments elaborated by the Institute include Principles on the Independence of the Judiciary and the Legal Profession, Principles on the Protection of the Rights of the Mentally Ill, and model treaties on the transfer of prisoners, transfer of criminal proceedings, extradition and enforcement of sentences.

The Institute has hosted conferences, seminars and meetings of experts in cooperation with the Division, as well as with the Centre for Human Rights. Over the last 22 years, it has conducted over 150 programmes, with the involvement of more than 12,000 jurors from 128 countries, and has cooperated with more than 40 non-governmental and governmental organizations. It has published 76 books.

The International Institute of
Higher Studies in Criminal Sciences
c/o Dr. Grazia Amato
Via Agati, 12
96100 Siracusa, Italy
Tel.: 39-931-35511/35611
Fax: 39-931-442605

The National Institute of Justice for the Prevention of Crime **NIJ**

In May 1995, the National Institute of Justice became the latest addition to the network of institutes affiliated or associated with the United Nations Crime Prevention and Criminal Justice Programme. The enabling Memorandum of Agreement was signed by the United States Department of Justice and the United Nations Office at Vienna at the Ninth Crime Congress, held in Cairo, Egypt. The NIJ, which promotes the exchange of criminal justice information worldwide, most notably over the Internet, joined the network after 25 years of operation.

As the research arm of the United States Department of Justice, the NIJ conducts studies of factors contributing to criminal behaviour, sponsors pilot projects in the criminal justice field and identifies emerging trends. Grants to criminal justice scholars support research in six key areas: reducing violent crime, reducing drug- and alcohol-related crime, reducing the consequences of crime, crime prevention programmes, improving law enforcement and the criminal justice system, and new technologies for law enforcement and criminal justice. The NIJ has sponsored studies on violence (particularly youth and family violence) and substance abuse, community policing, drug treatment courts, corrections and violence against women, and works with the US Centers for Disease Control and Prevention to address use of firearms by young people. Along with other US government agencies, the NIJ has developed an electronic information line, Partnerships Against Violence Network (PAVENT), for citizens and community groups seeking to locate anti-violence programmes in the US.

The Institute administers the International Document Exchange, with 105 members in 50 countries. To further promote the global exchange of information, the NIJ and the Mitre Corporation are developing, on behalf of the Crime Prevention and Criminal Justice Division, an Internet linkage between the United Nations criminological institutes. A special NIJ project, the International Rule of Law Online Clearinghouse Project, provides information on institution-building to the States of the former Soviet Union and to other countries. The Institute also administers a clearing-house of criminal justice information, the National Criminal Justice Reference Services (NCJRS), with a database and reference service that are available worldwide.

The Institute's extensive publications programme includes full reports of research and evalaution projects, conference proceedings and reports, the *NIJ Journal*, publications catalogs and drug use forecasting reports. All NIJ documents are published electronically, and the backlist is being converted to on-line availability.

Accessibility is through the NCJRS and its electronic bulletin board, via modem and the Internet. The NCJRS Justice Information Centre is accessible via the World Wide Web. In 1995, NIJ began publishing *JUSTINFO*, an electronic newsletter available on a subscription basis.

National Institute of Justice
c/o National Criminal Justice Reference Service
P.O. Box 600
Rockville, MD 29849-6000, USA
E-mail: ekline@ncjrs.aspensys.com

ISPAC   *The International Scientific and Professional Advisory Council*

ISPAC is a forum for bringing together non-governmental organizations and the professional and scientific community and channelling their combined contributions to the various components of the United Nations crime prevention and criminal justice programmes. The Advisory Council's objectives also include the promotion of technical assistance in priority areas by pooling the knowledge, expertise and experience available in NGOs and the professional and academic communities. ISPAC was established in 1991, pursuant to a Memorandum of Understanding between the Crime Prevention and Criminal Justice Branch and the Centro Nazionale di Prevenzione e Difesa Sociale, of Milan, Italy.

Among the Advisory Council's major contributions is its work in the area of transnational crime. The council organized the International Conference on Preventing and Controlling Money-Laundering and the Use of the Proceeds of Crime: a Global Approach, held in Courmayeur, Italy, in June 1994 (see Chapter 1). Publications include *Mafia Issues*, a report on the proceedings of an international symposium organized in 1993 in Oñate, Spain; proceedings of the Courmayeur money-laundering conference; and *Migration and Crime*, which includes a chapter on the role of crime syndicates in trafficking illegal aliens and laid the groundwork for discussion at a Ninth Crime Congress workshop.

ISPAC has organized meetings and published studies relating to other priority areas identified by ECOSOC: environmental damage and the role of criminal justice systems, elimination of violence against women, crime in urban areas, juvenile criminality, and victims' redress.

The functioning of ISPAC is made possible through the generosity of the Italian Government and the support of the Centro Nazionale, which serves as its secretariat.

The International Scientific and
Professional Advisory Council
c/o Centro Nazionale di Prevenzione e Difesa Sociale
3, Piazza Castello
20121 Milano, Italy
Tel.: 39-2-86-46-0714
Fax: 39-2-26-86-4427

Halte au Crime

Appendix

United Nations Standards, Guidelines and International Instruments

---

Standard Minimum Rules for the Treatment of Prisoners

Approved by the Economic and Social Council,
31 July 1957 (resolution 663 C I (XXIV)),
on the recommendation of the First Congress

Part 1:
Rules of General Application

Basic principle

The following rules are to be applied without discrimination on the grounds of race, colour, sex, language, religion, political opinions, national or social origin, property, birth or other status.

It is necessary, however, to respect religious beliefs of prisoners.

Register

A bound registration book shall be maintained with the identity, reasons for commitment and day and hour of admission and release of prisoners.

Separation of categories

Men and women in detention are to be held in separate facilities; likewise, untried and convicted prisoners, those imprisoned for civil offences and criminal offenders, and youths and adults shall be housed separately.

Accommodation

Cells for individuals should not be used to accommodate two or more persons overnight; dormitory facilities are to be supervised at night.

Cells and prison dormitories should provide adequate space, ventilation, lighting and sanitary facilities and are to be kept clean at all times.

Personal hygiene

Prisoners shall be provided with adequate water and toilet articles, and required to keep themselves clean.

Clothing and bedding

Prisoners not allowed to wear their own clothing are to be provided with an adequate and suitable outfit, with provisions for laundry and changes of clothes.

Prisoners outside an institution for an authorized purpose are to be allowed to wear their own clothing.

Every prisoner shall be provided with a separate bed and clean, separate and sufficient bedding.

Food

Wholesome, well-prepared food is to be provided prisoners at usual hours.

Drinking water shall be available whenever needed.

Exercise and sport

If not employed in outdoor work, every prisoner shall have at least one hour of exercise in the open air, weather permitting.

Young prisoners and others of suitable age and physique are to receive physical and recreational training.

Medical services

A medical officer with some knowledge of psychiatry is to be available to every institution.

Prisoners requiring specialized treatment are to be transferred to a civil hospital or appropriate facility.

A qualified dental officer shall be available to every prisoner.

Prenatal and post-natal care and treatment are to be provided by women's institutions; where nursing infants are allowed to remain with their mothers, a nursery staffed by qualified persons is needed.

Every prisoner shall be examined by the medical officer shortly after admission; prisoners suspected of contagious diseases are to be segregated.

The medical officer shall see all sick prisoners daily, along with those who complain of illness or are referred to his attention.

The medical officer is to report to the director on prisoners whose health is jeopardized by continued imprisonment and on the quality of the food, hygiene, bedding, clothing and physical regimen of the prisoners.

Discipline and punishment

Discipline shall be no more restrictive than what is necessary to ensure custody and order.

No prisoner shall be employed in a disciplinary capacity.

The types of conduct to be considered offences and punishments for them shall be set by law or regulation, and prisoners are to be allowed to defend themselves against charges.

Cruel, inhuman and/or degrading punishments, including corporal punishment and restriction to a dark cell, shall be prohibited.

The medical officer is to be consulted before implementing any punishment that may be prejudicial to the physical or mental health of a prisoner.

Instruments of restraint

Handcuffs, strait-jackets and other instruments of restraint are never to be applied as a punishment, and irons and chains are not to be used as means of restraint.

Information to and complaints by prisoners

Upon admission, prisoners shall be informed of the regulations they are to live by and of authorized channels for seeking information and making complaints.

Prisoners are to have the right to make complaints to the director of the institution, as well as to the central prison administration and the judicial authority, in the proper form but without censorship as to substance, and they are to have the opportunity to speak directly to an inspector of prisons outside the presence of institutional staff members.

Unless evidently frivolous, each complaint shall be replied to promptly.

Contact with the outside world

Prisoners are to be allowed regular contact with family and friends, by both correspondence and personal visits.

Prisoners who are foreign nationals shall be allowed communication with diplomatic and consular representatives of their State, or a State or international authority that has taken charge of their interests.

Prisoners are to be kept informed of current events and important items of news.

Books

Every institution shall maintain for the use of prisoners a library with recreational and instructional books.

Religion

If the institution contains a sufficient number of prisoners of the same religion, a qualified representative of each religion shall be appointed to hold services and pay pastoral visits.

No prisoner shall be refused access to a qualified representative of a religion, nor shall he be required to entertain a religious visit he objects to.

As far as is practicable, every prisoner is to be allowed to satisfy religious needs by attending services and possessing books of observance and instruction.

Retention of prisoners' property

Money, valuables and personal effects which prisoners are not allowed to keep in their possession are to be kept in safe custody until the prisoner's release.

Money or effects received by a prisoner from outside shall be treated the same way.

The medical officer is to decide what use shall be made of drugs or medicine a prisoner brings with him.

Notification of death, illness, transfer, etc.

The spouse or nearest relative shall be informed of the death, serious illness, injury or transfer of a prisoner to an institution for treatment of mental afflictions.

A prisoner is to be informed at once of the death or serious illness of any near relative. In cases of critical illness, the prisoner is to be allowed to visit that relative.

Every prisoner shall have the right to inform his family at once of his imprisonment or transfer.

Removal of prisoners

Prisoners being transferred are to be protected from insult, curiosity or publicity.

Conveyances which subject prisoners being transferred to unnecessary hardship shall be prohibited.

Transport is to be at the expense of the prison administration, and equal conditions shall obtain for all prisoners.

Institution personnel

The administration shall carefully select every grade of personnel and maintain in their minds and the public's the important social service they provide.

To these ends, pay, conditions and benefits shall be suitable to professional and exacting service.

Personnel are to be sufficiently educated, and to receive ongoing courses and training.

As far as possible, personnel should include psychiatric, social work and education professionals.

The director shall be a qualified administrator, retained on a full-time basis and residing on the premises or in the immediate vicinity.

Staff personnel are to be able to speak the language of the greatest number of prisoners, and to retain the services of an interpreter when necessary.

In larger institutions, at least one medical officer should reside on the premises or in the immediate vicinity.

In others, a medical officer shall visit daily and reside near enough to be available for emergencies.

In an institution for both men and women, the part set aside for women shall be under the authority of a woman officer, who shall have custody of the keys for that section.

Male officers shall enter the section for women only in the presence of a woman officer, and women prisoners shall be attended and treated only by women officers, without precluding male doctors and teachers from carrying out their duties.

Officers shall not use force except in self-defence, cases of attempted escape or resistance to an order based on law or regulation. Officers who have recourse to force must use no more than is strictly necessary and must report the incident immediately.

Prison officers are to receive physical training in the use of force. As a general rule, they should not carry weapons in the presence of prisoners.

Inspection

There shall be regular inspection of penal institutions.

Part 2:
Rules Applicable to Special Categories

Prisoners Under Sentence

Guiding principles

The prison system must not aggravate unnecessarily the suffering inherent in a prisoner's loss of self-determination and liberty.

Prisons should utilize all remedial, educational, medical and spiritual forms of assistance to treat the prisoner's needs and facilitate his return to society as a law-abiding member.

It is desirable to provide varying degrees of security according to the needs of different groups of prisoners. Open prisons that rely on self-discipline as opposed to physical restraint are preferable whenever possible.

Government or private agencies should be available for the aftercare of released prisoners.

Treatment

Treatment of prisoners under sentence shall be directed to achieve the capacity for law-abiding and self-supporting lives, utilizing professional services whenever possible.

The director shall receive full reports on the mental, social and physical status of prisoners under sentence of a suitable length directly after admission, keeping and updating this information in individual files.

Classification and individualization

To separate from others those prisoners who are likely to exercise a negative influence and to facilitate specialized treatment, prisoners are to be classified, and kept so far as possible in separate institutions or sections.

Privileges

Systems of privileges appropriate to different classes of prisoners shall be established to encourage proper conduct and secure the cooperation of prisoners in their treatment.

Work

Prison labour must not be of an afflictive nature.

All prisoners under sentence shall be required to work, unless determined to be physically or medically unfit.

So far as possible, the work should be of a full-time nature, conducive to vocational training and aligned with the choice of prisoners.

The interests and vocational training of prisoners are of greater importance than making a financial profit from their labour.

Institutional labour preferably will be directed by prison administrators rather than private contractors. When prisoners are employed in work not controlled by the administration, they should be under the supervision of the institution's personnel and the administration should be paid the normal wages for such work, unless the contractor is another government agency.

Precautions laid down to protect the safety and health of free workmen shall likewise be respected for prison labourers.

Maximum days and hours of work shall be fixed by law or regulation, taking into account local rules or customs regarding the employment of free workmen and to leave one rest day a week and sufficient time for education and treatment.

Prisoners are to be remunerated equitably, allowed to spend part of their earnings on approved articles for their own use, send a part to their families and set aside some in a savings fund.

Education and recreation

The ongoing education of prisoners is to be facilitated, and schooling of illiterates and youthful prisoners is to be considered compulsory.

Recreational and cultural activities are to be made available.

Social relations and after-care

Special attention shall be paid to maintaining and improving relations between a prisoner and his family.

The prisoner should be encouraged and assisted in cultivating relations with persons or extra-institutional agencies conducive to his rehabilitation and best interests after release.

Upon release, prisoners shall be provided with appropriate documents and identification papers, be suitably clothed and have sufficient means to reach their immediate destinations. They are to be assisted by services or agencies in locating suitable homes and work.

Representatives of such agencies shall have access to prisoners during their term of incarceration and be taken into consultation as to the future of each prisoner from the beginning of his sentence.

Insane and Mentally Abnormal Prisoners

Persons found to be insane are not to be detained in prisons.

Prisoners suffering from other mental abnormalities shall be observed and treated in specialized institutions under medical management and steps shall be taken to ensure the continuation of care after release.

Prisoners Under Arrest
or Awaiting Trial

Unconvicted prisoners are presumed to be innocent and shall be treated as such.

They shall be held separately from convicted prisoners, and the young kept separate from adults.

Prisoners awaiting trial are to sleep singly in separate rooms.

They may have food procured at their own expense; otherwise, the administration shall provide food.

An untried prisoner shall be allowed to wear his own clothing if clean and suitable; if he wears prison dress, it is to be different from that of convicted prisoners.

An untried prisoner may procure at his own expense or that of a third party books, publications and writing materials.

Treatment by an untried prisoner's own doctor or dentist is to be allowed under reasonable grounds, and if the prisoner is willing to pay for the expenses incurred.

An untried prisoner shall be allowed to inform his family of his detention immediately after arrest and communicate with and receive visits from family and friends.

He shall be allowed to apply for free legal aid where such aid is available, and to consult with his legal adviser regarding his defence. Such interviews may be within sight but not within the hearing of a police or institution official.

Civil Prisoners

Where law permits imprisonment for debt or by order of a non-criminal court, those so imprisoned shall be subjected to no greater restriction or severity than necessary for safe custody and good order. Their treatment shall be no less favourable than that accorded untried prisoners, with the reservation that they may be required to work.

Persons Arrested or Imprisoned Without Charges

Persons arrested or imprisoned without charge shall be accorded the same protection as other prisoners, without prejudice to the provisions of Article 9 of the International Covenant on Civil and Political Rights.

Declaration Against Torture and Other Cruel, Inhuman or Degrading Treatment or Punishment

Declaration Adopted by the
General Assembly, 9 December 1975

Any act of torture or other cruel, inhuman or degrading treatment or punishment is an offence to human dignity and a fundamental violation of human rights.

No State may permit or tolerate torture or other cruel, inhuman or degrading treatment or punishment. Exceptional circumstances, including state of war, internal political instability or public emergency, may not be invoked as justification of such acts.

Each State shall take take effective measures to prevent acts of torture and other cruel, inhuman or degrading treatment or punishment within its jurisdiction.

The training of law enforcement personnel and other public officials who may be responsible for persons deprived of their liberty shall ensure that full account is taken of the prohibition against torture and other cruel, inhuman or degrading treatment or punishment.

Each State shall systematically review interrogation methods and arrangements for the custody and treatment of prisoners with a view to preventing cases of torture or other cruel, inhuman or degrading treatment or punishment.

Each State shall ensure that all acts of torture are offences under its criminal law. The same shall apply to participation in, complicity in, incitement to or an attempt to commit torture.

Any person who alleges that he has been subjected to torture or other cruel, inhuman or degrading treatment or punishment by or at the instigation of a public official shall have the right to complain and have his case examined by competent authorities of the State.

Wherever there are reasonable grounds to believe that an act of torture has been committed, competent authorities shall carry out an impartial investigation even if there has been no formal complaint.

If investigation establishes that an act of torture appears to have been committed, criminal proceedings shall be instituted. If an allegation of other forms of cruel, inhuman or degrading treatment or punishment is considered to be well founded, criminal, disciplinary or other appropriate proceedings shall be instituted.

The victim of torture or other cruel, inhuman or degrading treatment or punishment shall be afforded redress and compensation under the law.

Any statement made under torture or as a result of other cruel, inhuman or degrading treatment or punishment may not be invoked as evidence against the person concerned or any other person in any proceedings.

An order from a superior officer or a public authority may not be invoked as a justification of torture.

No State Party shall expel, return or extradite a person to another State where there are substantial grounds for believing he would be in danger of torture.

Code of Conduct for Law Enforcement Officials

Adopted by the General Assembly,
17 December 1979 on the
recommendation of the Fifth Congress

All those who exercise police powers shall respect and protect human dignity and uphold the human rights of all persons.

Law enforcement officials shall fulfil the duty imposed on them by law by serving the community and protecting all persons against illegal acts.

Service to the community includes in particular assistance to those who by reason of personal, economic, social or other emergencies are in need of immediate aid.

Protection against illegal acts extends to the full range of prohibitions under penal statutes and to the conduct of persons not capable of incurring criminal liability.

Law enforcement officials may use force only when strictly necessary and only to the extent required for the performance of their duty.

The use of firearms is considered to be an extreme measure, not to be employed except when a suspected offender offers armed resistance or otherwise jeopardizes the lives of others.

Matters of a confidential nature in the possession of law enforcement officials shall be kept confidential, unless the performance of duty or the needs of justice strictly require otherwise

No law enforcement official may inflict, instigate or tolerate any act of torture or other cruel, inhuman or degrading treatment or punishment.

Law enforcement officials shall ensure the full protection of the health of persons in their custody and take immediate action to secure medical attention whenever required.

Law enforcement officials shall not commit any act of corruption and shall rigorously oppose and combat all such acts.

Law enforcement officials shall respect the law and this Code, and to the best of their capabilities prevent and oppose any violations of them.

If they believe that a violation of this Code has occurred or is about to occur, they shall report the matter to their superior authorities and, where necessary, to other appropriate authorities or governmental organs; as a last resort, and in accord with the laws and customs of their own countries, they may bring violations to the attention of the mass media.

Law enforcement officials who comply with the provisions of this Code deserve the respect, full support and cooperation of the community and of the law enforcement agency in which they serve.

Safeguards Guaranteeing Protection of the Rights of Those Facing the Death Penalty

Economic and Social Council resolution 1984/50, adopted 25 May 1984

In countries which have not abolished the death penalty, capital punishment may be imposed only for the most serious crimes, intentionally committed with lethal or extremely grave consequences.

Capital punishment may be imposed only for a crime for which the death penalty is prescribed by law at the time of its commission.

Persons below 18 years of age, pregnant women, new mothers or persons who have become insane shall not be sentenced to death.

Capital punishment may be imposed only when guilt is determined by clear and convincing evidence leaving no room for an alternative explanation of the facts.

Capital punishment may be carried out only after a final judgement rendered by a competent court allowing all possible safeguards to the defendant, including adequate legal assistance.

Anyone sentenced to death shall have the right of appeal to a court of higher jurisdiction.

Anyone sentenced to death shall have the right to seek pardon or commutation of sentence.

Capital punishment shall not be carried out pending any appeal, recourse procedure or proceeding relating to pardon or commutation of the sentence.

Where capital punishment occurs, it shall be carried out so as to inflict the minimum possible suffering.

The Milan Plan of Action

Adopted by the Seventh Crime Congress,
Milan, 26 August-6 September 1985,
and endorsed by the General Assembly
in resolution 40/32

Possessing national and international dimensions, the problem of crime demands a concerted response from the community of nations to reduce opportunities for the commission of crimes and to address relevant socio-economic factors, such as poverty, inequality and unemployment. Unbalanced or inadequately planned development contributes to an increase in criminality, and the criminal justice system should be fully responsive to diverse and evolving political, economic and social systems.

Recommendations

Governments should give high priority to crime prevention and criminal justice through strengthening appropriate mechanisms and allocation of adequate resources.

Action-oriented programmes and projects should be undertaken in the field with the assistance of full bilateral and multilateral cooperation.

Research and database capabilities of the United Nations and Member States should be strengthened, with special attention to possible interrelationships between criminality and specific aspects of development, such as population structure and growth, housing, migration, urbanization and employment opportunities.

Further study of crime in relation to human rights and fundamental freedoms is needed for investigation of new and traditional forms of crime.

Member States should adopt concrete and urgent measures to eradicate racial discrimination and other forms of oppression, particularly apartheid.

Priority must be given to combating terrorism in all its forms and to coordinated action by the international community in that regard.

Launching a major effort to control and eventually eradicate illicit drug trafficking and abuse is imperative.

To further the improvement of criminal justice systems, the United Nations should facilitate the exchange of information and experience between Member States and should undertake study and policy research.

Non-governmental organizations should continue to be effectively involved in United Nations efforts in the field.

The UN Secretary-General is requested to review the United Nations work programmes in crime prevention and control with special attention to improving coordination of the Organization's activities.

UN regional and interregional institutes should be strengthened and their programmes reinforced. Immediate action should be taken to establish the regional institute for Africa.

UN capacities to extend technological cooperation to developing countries should be reinforced.

Member States should intensify their efforts, including in the area of education, to develop the widest possible participation in preventing and combating crime.

Guiding Principles for Crime Prevention and Criminal Justice in the Context of Development and a New Economic Order

Adopted by the Seventh Crime Congress,
Milan, 26 August-6 September 1985,
and endorsed by the General Assembly
in resolution 40/32

Changes in national economic and social structures should be accompanied by appropriate criminal justice reforms.

International cooperation should be encouraged to foster balanced economic development, through restructuring of the international economic system, with due emphasis on crime prevention and the proper functioning of criminal justice systems.

Policies for crime prevention and criminal justice should take into account the structural causes, including socio-economic causes, of injustice.

New directions and approaches should be explored regarding crime-related concepts, measures, procedures and institutions.

Member States should refrain from committing acts aimed at harming the development of other countries and should assist each other in crime prevention and criminal justice efforts.

Crime prevention as a global phenomenon should not be confined to common criminality, but should also address especially harmful crimes, including economic crime, environmental offences, illegal drug trafficking, terrorism, apartheid and other comparable crimes.

Special protection against criminal negligence should be ensured in matters concerning public health, labour conditions, exploitation of natural resources and the environment and the provision of consumer goods and services.

Laws governing the functioning of business enterprises should be reviewed and strengthened as necessary, and consideration should be given to having complex cases of economic crime heard by judges familiar with business procedures.

States should give due consideration to making institutions as well as individuals criminally responsible.

More appropriate penalties for economic crimes should be established where existing measures do not correspond to the gravity of those offenses.

Economic penalties should be graded to ensure that they are equally exemplary for both poor and wealthy offenders.

Measures should be taken to provide crime victims with effective legal protection, including compensation for damages resulting from crime.

Crime prevention strategies should be formulated in relation to the socio-economic context, the society's developmental stage and its traditions and customs.

Legal systems, including criminal justice, should be instrumental in promoting beneficial and equitable development. While protecting human rights and promoting social justice, improvements in crime prevention effectiveness and criminal justice policies should be encouraged through consideration of alternatives to incarceration and judicial intervention.

Equality, fairness and equity in the processes of law enforcement, prosecution, sentencing and treatment should be ensured so as to avoid discriminatory practices based on socio-economic, cultural, ethnic, national or political backgrounds, sex or material means.

Safeguards should be established concerning the use of modern technology and computer systems so as to avoid possible violations of the right to privacy and other human rights.

International cooperation should be "less cumbersome and more effective" in areas such as extradition of offenders, investigative and judicial assistance and transfer of foreign prisoners. Technical and scientific cooperation should be increased.

Basic Principles on the Independence of the Judiciary

Adopted by the Seventh Crime Congress,
Milan, 26 August-6 September 1985,
and endorsed by the General Assembly
in resolution 40/32

The independence of the judiciary shall be guaranteed by the State and enshrined in the constitution or law of the country.

The judiciary shall decide matters before them with impartiality on the basis of facts, in accordance with the law, without any improper influences or pressures.

Everyone shall have the right to be tried by ordinary courts or tribunals using established legal procedures. Tribunals that do not use established legal procedures shall not be created to displace the jurisdiction belonging to ordinary courts.

Members of the judiciary, like other citizens, are entitled to freedom of expression, belief, association and assembly; however, judges shall always conduct themselves in a manner so as to preserve the dignity of their office and the impartiality and independence of the judiciary.

Persons selected for judicial office shall be individuals of integrity and ability with appropriate training or qualifications in law. In selection of judges, there shall be no discrimination on the basis of race, colour, sex, religion, political or other opinion, national or social origin, property, birth or status.

The term of office and conditions of service for judges shall be secured by law. Judges shall have guaranteed tenure until retirement or expiration of their term of office.

Assignment of cases to judges is an internal matter of judicial administration.

The judiciary shall be bound by professional secrecy concerning their deliberations and shall not be compelled to testify on such matters.Without prejudice to any disciplinary procedure or to any right of appeal or compensation from the State, judges should enjoy personal immunity from civil suits for monetary damages for improper acts or omissions in the exercise of their judicial functions.A judge shall have the right to a fair hearing on charges or complaints against her/him. Judges shall be subject to suspension or removal only for reasons of incapacity or behaviour that renders them unfit to discharge their duties.

Decisions in disciplinary, suspension or removal proceedings should be subject to an independent review, except concerning decisions by the highest court and those of the legislature in impeachment or similar proceedings.

Model Agreement on the Transfer of Foreign Prisoners and Recommendations on the Treatment of Foreign Prisoners

Adopted by the Seventh Crime Congress,
Milan, 26 August-6 September 1985,
and endorsed by the General Assembly
in resolution 40/32

The social resettlement of offenders should be promoted by quickly facilitating the return of persons convicted of crime abroad to their home country to serve their sentence.

Prisoner transfer should take place where the offence in question is punishable by deprivation of liberty in both sending (sentencing) and receiving (administering) countries. A transfer may be requested by either the sentencing or the administering State.

A transfer shall be dependent on the consent of both States and the prisoner as well. The administering State should be given the opportunity to verify the free consent of the prisoner.

At the time of request for a transfer, as a general rule, the prisoner shall have at least six months of the sentence remaining to be served.

The administering State shall either continue enforcement of the sentence or convert the sentence to one prescribed by its law for a corresponding offence.

In the case of continued enforcement, the administering State shall be bound by the sentence determined by the sentencing State. It may, however, adapt the sanction to the punishment prescribed by its own law for the offence, but a sanction involving deprivation of liberty shall not be converted to a pecuniary sanction.

The administering State shall be bound by the findings of the sentencing State, which has the sole competence for review of the sentence.

Costs incurred as a result of a transfer shall be borne by the administering State, unless otherwise decided by both States.

Both the sentencing and administering States shall be competent to grant pardon and amnesty.

Recommendations on the Treatment of Foreign Prisoners

Foreign prisoners should have the same access as national prisoners to education, work and vocational training.

Foreign prisoners should be eligible for alternative measures to imprisonment according to the same principles as nationals.

The religious precepts and customs of foreign prisoners should be respected.

Foreign prisoners should be informed, in a language they understand, of the prison regime and regulations as well as their right to request contact with consular authorities. Proper assistance should be given in dealings with medical or programme staff and concerning such matters as complaints, special diets and religious representation and counselling.

Contacts should be facilitated between foreign prisoners and their families and with humanitarian international organizations.

Standard Minimum Rules for the Administration of Juvenile Justice

Adopted by the General Assembly,
29 November 1985 (resolution 40/33),
on the recommendation of the
Seventh Congress

Part 1:
General Principles

Fundamental perspectives

Member States shall seek to further the well-being of juveniles and their families.

Member States shall try to develop conditions to ensure meaningful lives in the community for juveniles.

Sufficient attention should be given to positive measures involving mobilization of resources, such as the family, volunteers and community groups, to promote the well-being of juveniles.

Juvenile justice shall be an integral part of the national development process of each country.

Age of criminal responsibility

In legal systems recognizing the concept of an age of criminal responsibility for juveniles, such an age level shall not be fixed too low, bearing in mind emotional, mental and physical maturity.

Aims of juvenile justice

Any reaction by the juvenile justice system to juvenile offenders shall be in proportion to both the offenders and the offence.

Scope of discretion

Appropriate scope for the exercise of discretionary power shall be allowed at all stages of legal proceedings affecting juveniles.

Efforts shall be made to ensure sufficient accountability at all stages in the exercise of such discretion.

Rights of juveniles

Basic procedural safeguards, such as the presumption of innocence, the right to be notified of charges, the right to remain silent, the right to counsel, the right to the presence of a parent or guardian, the right to confront and cross-examine witnesses and the right to appeal, shall be guaranteed at all stages of proceedings.

Protection of privacy

The juvenile's right to privacy shall be respected at all stages.

Part 2:
Investigation and Prosecution

Initial contact

Upon the apprehension of a juvenile, parents or guardians shall be notified as soon as possible.

A judge or other competent official or body shall consider the issue of release without delay.

Diversion

Consideration shall be given to dealing with juvenile offenders without resort to trial, and any diversion to appropriate community or other services shall require consent of the juvenile or parents.

Police officers dealing frequently or exclusively with juveniles shall be specially instructed and trained.

Detention pending trial

Detention pending trial shall be used only as a last resort and for the shortest possible period of time.

When possible, detention pending trial shall be replaced by alternative measures, such as close supervision or placement with a family.

Juveniles under detention pending trial shall be kept separate from adults.

While in custody, juveniles shall receive care, protection and all necessary assistance that they may require in view of their age, sex and personality.

Part 3:
Adjudication and Disposition

Competent authority to adjudicate

Where the case of a juvenile offender has not been diverted, she or he shall be dealt with by the competent authority according to the principles of a fair trial.

Judicial proceedings shall be conducted in an atmosphere of understanding, allowing the juvenile free self-expression.

Legal counsel, parents and guardians

Throughout the proceedings, juveniles shall have the right to be represented by a legal advisor. Parents or guardians shall be entitled to participate, unless their exclusion is required in the best interests of the juvenile concerned.

Social inquiry reports

Prior to sentencing and final disposition, the background and circumstances of the offender shall be properly investigated.

Guiding principles in adjudication and disposition

Regarding adjudication and disposition, the reaction taken shall always be in proportion not only to the circumstances and gravity of the offence, but also to the needs and circumstances of the juvenile and society.

Restrictions on the personal liberty of juveniles shall be imposed only after careful consideration and shall be limited to the minimum. Deprivation of liberty shall not be imposed except in cases of serious acts involving violence against another person or of persistence in committing other serious offenses.

Capital punishment shall not be imposed for any crime committed by juveniles.

Juveniles shall not be subjected to corporal punishment.

Various disposition measures

To provide flexibility so as to avoid institutionalization to the greatest extent possible, a large variety of disposition measures should be made available, including probation, community service, supervision, financial penalties, group counselling, foster care, etc.

No juvenile shall be removed from parental supervision unless due to necessary circumstances.

Least possible use of institutionalization

The placement of a juvenile in an institution shall always be a disposition of last resort and for the minimum necessary period.

Avoidance of unnecessary delay

Each case shall be handled expeditiously.

Records

Records of juvenile offenders shall be kept strictly confidential and shall be limited to duly authorized personnel.

Records of juvenile offenders shall not be used in adult proceedings in subsequent cases involving the same offender.

Need for professionalism and training

Professional education, in-service training, refresher courses and other modes of instruction shall be utilized.

Juvenile justice personnel shall reflect the diversity of juveniles in contact with the justice system. Efforts shall be made to ensure fair representation of women and minorities.

Part 4:
Non-institutional Treatment

Provision of needed assistance

Efforts shall be made to provide necessary assistance, such as lodging, education, vocational training and employment, to facilitate the rehabilitation process. Help from volunteers shall also be sought.

Part 5:
Institutional Treatment

Objectives of institutional treatment

Measures shall be taken within institutions for juveniles to provide care, protection, education and vocational skills to assist offenders in assuming constructive and productive roles in society.

Juveniles in institutions shall be kept separate from adults, and special attention shall be given to young female offenders.

Conditional release from institutions with appropriate support and assistance shall be used to the greatest extent possible.

Part 6:
Research, Planning, Policy Formulation and Evaluation

Semi-institutional arrangements

Efforts shall be made to provide semi-institutional arrangements, such as halfway houses, educational homes and daytime training centres, to assist juveniles in their re-integration into society.

Research as a basis for planning, policy formulation and evaluation

Efforts shall be made to review and appraise periodically the causes and problems of juvenile delinquency and crime and the needs of juveniles in custody.

Declaration of Basic Principles of Justice for Victims of Crime and the Abuse of Power

Approved by the General Assembly, 29 November 1985 (resolution 40/34), on the recommendation of the Seventh Congress

Victims should be treated with compassion and respect for their dignity and are entitled to prompt redress for harm caused.

Judicial and administrative mechanisms should be established and strengthened to enable victims to obtain redress.

Victims should be informed of their role and the timing and progress of their cases.

The views and concerns of victims should be presented and considered at appropriate stages of the process.

Steps should be taken to minimize delay and inconvenience to victims, ensure their privacy and protect them from intimidation and retaliation.

Offenders should, where appropriate, make restitution to victims or their families or dependants. Where public officials have violated criminal laws, victims should receive restitution from the State.

When compensation is not fully available from the offender, States should provide compensation to victims or their families in cases of significant physical or mental injury.

Victims should receive the necessary material, medical, psychological and social assistance through governmental and voluntary means.

Police, justice, social service and other personnel concerned should receive training to sensitize them to the needs of victims.

States should consider incorporating into national law norms proscribing abuses of power, including political and economic power. They should also provide remedies to victims of such abuses, including restitution and compensation.

Standard Minimum Rules for Non-Custodial Measures

Adopted by the General Assembly as resolution 45/110 on the recommendation of the Eighth Congress

General Principles

Fundamental aims

The Standard Minimum Rules are basic principles to promote the use of non-custodial measures and establish minimum safeguards for persons subject to alternatives to imprisonment.

The Rules are intended to promote greater community involvement in the management of criminal justice and to promote among offenders a sense of responsibility towards society.

The scope of non-custodial measures

Relevant provisions are applied to all persons subject to prosecution, trial or terms of sentencing. The criminal justice system should provide a wide range of non-custodial measures, from pretrial to post-sentencing dispositions, to allow flexibility while maintaining a capacity for consistent sentencing.

Use of non-custodial measures should be part of the movement towards depenalization, decriminalization, the principle of minimum intervention and use of informal community measures, instead of interfering or delaying efforts in those directions.

Legal safeguards

Discretion by judicial or other competent independent authority is to be exercised at all stages of proceedings to ensure full accountability and accordance with the rule of law.

Non-custodial measures imposing an obligation on the offender, applied before or instead of formal procedings or trial, shall require the offender's consent.

The offender is entitled to make a request or complaint regarding implementation of non-custodial measures, and appropriate machinery shall be provided for the redress of any grievance related to violation of internationally recognized human rights.

Non-custodial measures shall not involve medical or psychological experimentation or undue risk of injury and shall respect the dignity and privacy of the offender.

Pre-Trial Stage

Pre-trial dispositions

Where appropriate and compatible with the legal system, the police and prosecution should discharge the offender if they consider that protection of society, crime prevention and respect for the law and rights of victims will not be served by proceeding with the case. A set of established criteria shall be developed for deciding the appropriateness of discharge. For minor cases the prosecutor may impose suitable non-custodial measures.

Avoidance of pre-trial detention

Pre-trial detention is to be used as a last resort in criminal proceedings, with due regard for the investigation of the alleged offence and protection of society and the victim, and the offender shall have the right to appeal its use.

Alternatives to pre-trial detention shall be employed at as early a stage as possible.

Trial and Sentencing Stage

Social inquiry reports

When available, judicial authority may make use of a factual, unbiased report by a competent official or agency that contains social information about the offender relevant to that person's pattern of offending and information and recommendations relevant to sentencing.

Sentencing dispositions

In deciding a sentence, the judicial authority is to consider the rehabilitative needs of the offenders, the protection of society and the interests of the victim.

Sentencing authorities may dispose of cases in the following ways:

a) Verbal sanctions, such as admonition, reprimand and warning;

b) Conditional discharge;

c) Status penalties;

d) Economic sanctions and monetary penalties, such as fines and day-fines;

e) Confiscation or an expropriation order;

f) Restitution to the victim or a compensation order;

g) Suspended or deferred sentence;

h) Probation and judicial supervision;

i) A community service order;

j) Referral to an attendance centre;

k) House arrest;

l) Any other mode of non-institutional treatment;

m) Some combination of the measures listed above.

Post-Sentencing Stage

The competent authority shall have at its disposal a wide range of post-sentencing alternatives to avoid institutionalization and assist offenders in their early reintegration into society.

Post-sentencing disposition may include:

a) Furlough and halfway houses;

b) Work or education release;

c) Various forms of parole;

d) Remission;

e) Pardon.

Release from an institution to a non-custodial programme shall be considered at the earliest possible stage.

Implementation of Non-Custodial Measures

Supervision

The purpose of supervision is to reduce re-offending and assist the offender's integration into society.

Offenders should, when needed, be provided with psychological, social and material assistance and with opportunities to strengthen links with the community and facilitate reintegration.

Duration

Duration of non-custodial measures shall not exceed the period established by the competent authority in accordance with the law.

Provision may be made for early termination if the offender responds favourably.

Conditions

In determining the conditions to be observed by the offender, account should be taken of the needs of society and the needs and rights of the offender and the victim.

Conditions to be observed shall be practical, precise and as few as possible, aimed at reducing the likelihood of relapse by the offender and taking into account the needs of the victim.

At the beginning of non-custodial measures, the offender shall receive an explanation, orally and in writing, of the conditions governing the measures.

Conditions may be modified by the competent authority in accord with progress made by the offender.

Treatment process

In appropriate cases, case-work, group therapy, residential programmes and specialized treatment should be developed to meet the needs of offenders.

Treatment should be conducted by professionals with suitable training and experience.

Efforts should be made to understand the offender's background, personality, aptitude, intelligence, values and the circumstances leading to commission of the offence.

The community and social support systems may be involved in application of non-custodial measures.

Case-load assignments are to be maintained at a manageable level.

For each offender, a case record is to be maintained and established.

Discipline and breach of conditions

A breach of the conditions to be observed may result in modification or revocation of the non-custodial measure, although it should not automatically do so.

Modification or revocation shall be made by the competent authority after careful examination of the facts.

In such event, a suitable alternative is to be sought. Imprisonment may be imposed only in the absence of other suitable alternatives.

The power to arrest and detain the offender in cases where there is a breach of the conditions shall be prescribed by law.

The offender shall have the right to appeal modification or revocation of the non-custodial measure.

Staff

Recruitment

Persons appointed to apply non-custodial measures should be personally and professionally suitable, and there shall be no discrimination on the grounds of race, colour, sex, age, language, religion, political or other opinion, national or social origin, property, birth or other status in their recruitment.

Adequate salary and benefits and opportunity for professional growth and career advancement should be provided.

Staff training

Before entering on duty, staff shall be given training in the nature and various modalities of non-custodial measures and the purposes of supervision.

Staff shall maintain and improve their knowledge by entering in-service training and refresher courses.

Volunteers and Other Community Resources

Public participation

Public participation should be encouraged as it is a major resource and an important factor in improving ties between offenders undergoing non-custodial measures, their families and the community.

It should be regarded as an opportunity for members of the community to contribute to the protection of their society.

Public understanding and cooperation

Conferences, seminars, symposia and other activities should be organized to stimulate awareness of the need for public participation in the application of non-custodial measures.

All forms of mass media should be utilized to help create a constructive public attitude.

Volunteers

Volunteers shall be carefully screened and recruited on the basis of aptitude for and interest in the work involved, receive proper training and have access to support and counselling from, and the opportunity to consult with, the competent authority.

Volunteers should be insured against accident, injury and public liability and reimbursed for authorized expenditures. Public recognition should be extended to them.

Research, Planning, Policy Formulation and Evaluation

Research on non-custodial treatment of offenders and the problems that confront clients, practitioners, the community and policy makers should be carried out regularly and relevant research and information mechanisms built into the criminal justice system's collection and analysis of data.

Suitable mechanisms should be evolved for linkages between services responsible for non-custodial measures and other branches of the criminal justice system, social development and welfare agencies, both governmental and non-governmental, in such fields as health, housing, education and labour, and with the mass media.

Efforts shall be made to promote scientific cooperation between countries in the field of non-institutional treatment. Research, training, technical assistance and the exchange of information should be strengthened through the United Nations regional and interregional institutes, in close collaboration with the Crime Prevention and Criminal Justice Branch of the United Nations Secretariat.

Guidelines for the Prevention of Juvenile Delinquency

Adopted by the General Assembly as resolution 45/112 on the recommendation of the Eighth Congress

Fundamental Principles

The prevention of juvenile delinquency is an essential part of crime prevention in society. By engaging in lawful, socially useful activities and adopting a humanistic orientation, young persons can develop non-criminogenic attitudes.

Prevention of juvenile delinquency requires efforts by the entire society to ensure the harmonious development of adolescents, with respect for and promotion of their personality from early childhood.

A child-centred orientation should be pursued. Young persons should have an active role and partnership within society and should not be considered mere objects of socialization or control.

Progressive delinquency prevention policies should avoid criminalizing a child for behaviour that does not cause serious damage to the development of the child or harm to others. Policies and measures should involve:

a) Educational and other opportunities to serve as a supportive framework for the personal development of young persons, particularly those who are endangered or at social risk;

b) Specialized philosophies and approaches for prevention on the basis of laws, processes, institutions, facilities and a service delivery

network aimed at reducing motivation, need
and opportunity for infractions;

c) Official intervention pursued in the overall
interest of the young person and guided by
fairness and equity;

d) Safeguarding the well-being, development,
rights and interests of all young persons;

e) Consideration that youthful behaviour that does
not conform to overall social norms and values
is often part of the maturation and growth process
and tends to disappear spontaneously with the
transition to adulthood;

f) Awareness that labelling a young person as
"deviant", "delinquent" or "pre-delinquent" often
contributes to a pattern of undesirable behaviour.

Community-based services should be developed for the prevention of juvenile delinquency, particularly where no agencies have
yet been established. Formal agencies of social control should be
utilized only as a last resort.

Scope of the Guidelines

These Guidelines should be interpreted and implemented within
the framework of all United Nations instruments and norms
relating to the rights, interests and well-being of all children and
young persons, and implemented in the context of the economic, social and cultural conditions in each Member State.

General Prevention

Comprehensive prevention plans should be instituted at every
level of government and include the following:

a) In-depth analyses of the problem and inventories
of programmes, services, facilities and resources;

b) Well-defined responsibilities for involved
agencies, institutions and personnel;

c) Mechanisms for coordination of efforts between
governmental and non-governmental agencies;

d) Policies, programmes and strategies based on prognostic studies and continuous monitoring and evaluation;

e) Methods for reducing opportunities to commit delinquent acts;

f) Community involvement through a wide range of services and programmes;

g) Interdisciplinary cooperation between national, state, provincial and local governments, with involvement of the private sector, the citizenry, and labour, child-care, health, education, social, law enforcement and judicial agencies;

h) Youth participation in prevention policies and processes;

i) Specialized personnel at all levels.

Socialization Processes

Family

Since the family is the central unit responsible for the primary socialization of children, efforts should be made to preserve the integrity of the family and extended family, including adequate day-care facilities.

Families should be provided with necessary assistance in resolving conditions of instability or conflict.

When a settled family environment is lacking and efforts of the community and extended family to assist parents have failed, foster care and adoption should be considered. Such placements should replicate, to the extent possible, a stable family environment and avoid the problem of "foster drift".

Special attention should be given to children affected by rapid and uneven economic, social and cultural change, in particular the children of migrant and refugee families, and innovative and socially constructive modalities for the socialization of children should be designed.

Measures should be taken to help families learn about parental roles and obligations and encourage their involvement in family and community-based activities.

Education

Governments are under an obligation to make public education accessible to all young persons.

Educational systems should devote attention to the following:

> a) Teaching basic values and developing respect for the child's own culture, for the social values of the country in which the child is living, for civilizations different from the child's own and for human rights and fundamental freedoms;

> b) Promoting development of the personality and talents of young people to their fullest potential;

> c) Involvement of young persons as active participants rather than mere objects in the educational process;

> d) Activities that foster a sense of identity with the school and the community;

> e) Encouragement of young persons to understand diverse views and opinions;

> f) Information and guidance regarding vocational opportunities and career development;

> g) Avoidance of harsh disciplinary measures, particularly corporal punishment.

Educational systems should work with parents, community organizations and agencies concerned with young persons.

Young persons and their families should be informed about the law and their rights and responsibilities, as well as the universal value system, including United Nations instruments.

Particular attention should be extended to young persons who are at social risk, utilizing specialized programmes and educational materials.

Attention is also to be given to policies and strategies for the prevention of alcohol, drug and other substance abuse.

Schools should serve as resource and referral centres for medical, counselling and other services to young persons, particularly those with special needs or suffering from abuse or neglect.

Teachers, adults and students need to be sensitized to the problems and perceptions of young people belonging to underprivileged, minority or low-income groups.

School systems should attempt to meet and promote the highest standards, and regular monitoring and evaluation by appropriate professional organizations should be ensured.

Extra-curricular activities of interest to young persons should be developed by school systems in cooperation with community groups.

Special assistance should be given to students who find it difficult to comply with attendance codes and to "drop-outs".

School policies and rules should be fair, and students should be represented in school policy, including policy on discipline and decision-making.

Community

Community-based services which respond to the interests of young persons, including community development centres and recreational facilities, should be developed and strengthened.

Adequate shelter should be provided for young persons who are no longer able to live at home or have no homes.

Services should be provided to deal with the difficult transition of young persons to adulthood, including special programmes for young drug abusers that emphasize care, counselling, assistance and therapy.

Voluntary organizations serving young people are to receive financial and other support.

Local youth organizations should be created and strengthened and given participatory status in management of community affairs. They should encourage youth to organize collective and voluntary projects, particularly to benefit young persons in need of assistance.

Government agencies are to provide necessary services for homeless or street children.

A wide range of recreational facilities and services of interest to young persons should be established and made easily accessible.

Mass media

The mass media should ensure that young persons have access to information from a diversity of national and international sources.

It should portray the positive contributions of young people to society.

Information on services, facilities and opportunities for young persons should be disseminated.

Mass media in general, and film and television in particular, should minimize the portrayal of pornography, drugs and violence, display violence and exploitation unfavourably, avoid demeaning and degrading presentations, especially of children, women and interpersonal relations, and promote egalitarian principles and roles.

The mass media should use its power for drug abuse prevention by relaying consistent messages through a balanced approach and by promoting effective drug awareness campaigns.

Social Policy

Government agencies should give high priority to plans and programmes for young persons and provide sufficient funds and resources for adequate medical and mental health care, nutrition, housing, and substance abuse prevention.

Institutionalization of young persons should be a measure of last resort and for the minimum necessary period. Criteria for intervention of this sort should be strictly defined and limited to situations where the child or young person:

> a) has suffered harm inflicted by parents or guardians;

> b) has been sexually or physically abused;

> c) has been neglected, abandoned or exploited by the parents or guardians;

> d) is threatened by physical or moral danger due to the behaviour of parents; or

> e) is in jeopardy of serious physical or psychological danger manifested in his or her own

behaviour and neither the parents or guardians
nor the juvenile himself or herself can meet
the danger by means other than institutionalization.

Government agencies should provide young persons with the
opportunity of continuing in full-time education, funded by the
State where the parents or guardians are unable to support the
young persons, and of receiving work experience.

Programmes to prevent delinquency should be planned and
developed on the basis of scientific research and periodically
monitored, evaluated and adjusted.

Scientific information should be disseminated to professionals
and the public at large about the sort of behaviour or situation
which indicates or may result in victimization or abuse of young
persons.

Generally, participation of young persons in programmes should
be voluntary, and young persons should be involved in formulation and implementation of youth programmes.

Governments should take measures to prevent domestic violence
against young persons and ensure fair treatment for victims.

Legislation and Juvenile
Justice Administration

Specific laws and procedures should be enacted to protect the
rights and well-being of all young persons, including legislation
against the victimization, abuse, exploitation and use for criminal activity of children and young persons.

No child or young person should be subjected to harsh or degrading correction measures or punishment at home, in schools or in
any other institution.

Legislation and enforcement should restrict and control accessibility of weapons to children and young persons.

Any conduct not considered an offence or penalized if committed by an adult should not be considered an offence or penalized
if committed by a young person.

Law enforcement personnel and other relevant personnel, of both sexes, should be trained to respond to the special needs of young persons and be made familiar with programmes and referral possibilities for the diversion of young persons from the justice system.

Legislation should protect children and young persons from drug abuse and drug traffickers.

Research Policy Development and Coordination

Multidisciplinary and interdisciplinary efforts should be made to promote interaction between economic, social, educational and health agencies and services, the justice system, youth, community and development agencies and other relevant institutions.

Exchange of information and experience and technical and scientific cooperation in practical and policy-related matters should be intensified at the national, regional and international levels and within the United Nations system.

The United Nations Secretariat should play an active role in research, formulation of policy options and review of practical implementation and as a source of reliable information.

Rules for the Protection of Juveniles Deprived of their Liberty

Adopted by the General Assembly as resolution 45/113 on the recommendation of the Eighth Congress

Fundamental Perspectives

The juvenile justice system should uphold the rights and safety and promote the physical and mental well-being of juveniles.

Imprisonment should be used as a last resort, should be in accord with the principles and procedures in these Rules and in the Standard Minimum Rules for the Administration of Juvenile

Justice, and should be for the minimum necessary period. The length of the sanction should be determined by judicial authority, without precluding the possibility of early release.

The Rules are designed to establish minimum standards accepted by the United Nations for the protection of juveniles deprived of their liberty and serve as convenient standards of reference to professionals involved in the juvenile justice system. They should be made available to juvenile justice personnel in their national languages. Where appropriate, States should incorporate the Rules into their legislation or amend it accordingly and provide effective remedies for their breach, including compensation when injuries are inflicted on juveniles.

Competent authorities should seek to increase the awareness of the public that care of detained juveniles and preparation for their return to society is a social service of great importance. To this end, contacts between the juveniles and the local community should be fostered.

Scope and Application of the Rules

The following definitions apply:

> a) A juvenile is every person under the age of 18. The age limit below which it should not be permitted to deprive a child of liberty is to be determined by law.
>
> b) The deprivation of liberty means any form of detention or imprisonment or placement of a person in a public or private custodial setting, from which this person is not permitted to leave at will, ordered by any judicial, administrative or public authority.

Deprivation of liberty should be effected in conditions and circumstances which ensure respect for the human rights of juveniles. Detained juveniles should be guaranteed meaningful activities and programmes which promote health and self-respect, foster their sense of responsibility and encourage their development as potential members of society.

Detained juveniles are not to be denied for any reasons related to their status civil, economic, political, social or cultural rights to which they are entitled under national or international law and which are compatible with the deprivation of their liberty, such as social security benefits, freedom of association and, upon reaching the minimum age established by law, the right to marry.

Protection of the individual rights of juveniles with special regard to the legality of the execution of the detention measures shall be ensured by the competent authority, while the objectives of social integration should be secured by regular inspections and other controls carried out according to international standards and national laws and regulations by a duly constituted body authorized to visit the juveniles and not belonging to the detention facility.

The Rules apply to all types and forms of detention facilities in which juveniles are deprived of their liberty.

The Rules are to be implemented in the context of the economic, social and cultural conditions prevailing in each Member State.

Juveniles Under Arrest or Awaiting Trial

Juveniles who are detained under arrest or awaiting trial ("untried") are presumed innocent and shall be treated as such. Detention before trial shall be avoided and limited to exceptional circumstances. All efforts shall be made to apply alternative measures. When preventive detention is nevertheless used, juvenile courts and investigative bodies shall give the highest priority to expeditious processing of such cases to ensure the shortest possible duration of detention. Untried detainees should be separated from convicted juveniles.

The conditions under which an untried juvenile is detained should include, but not necessarily be limited to, the following:

a) Juveniles should have the right of legal counsel and be enabled to apply for free legal aid, where such aid is available, and to communicate regularly and confidentially with their legal advisers.

b) Juveniles should be provided, where possible, with opportunities to pursue work, with remuneration, and continue education or training, but should not be required to do so. Work, education or training should not cause the continuation of detention.

c) Juveniles should receive and retain materials for their leisure and recreation as are compatible with the interests of the administration of justice.

The Management of Juvenile Facilities

Records

All reports, including legal records, medical records, records of disciplinary proceedings and all other documents relating to the form, content and details of treatment, should be placed in a confidential individual file. Where possible, every juvenile should have the right to contest any fact or opinion contained in his or her file. In order to exercise this right, there should be procedures that allow an appropriate third party to consult the file on request. Upon release, the records of juveniles shall be sealed and, at an appropriate time, expunged.

No juvenile should be received in any detention facility without a valid commitment order of a judicial, administrative or other public authority. No juvenile should be detained in any facility where there is no such register.

Admission, registration, movement and transfer

In every place where juveniles are detained, a complete and secure record of the following information should be kept concerning each juvenile:

> a) Information on the identity of the juvenile;
>
> b) The fact of and reasons for commitment and the authority thereof;
>
> c) The day and hour of admission, transfer and release;
>
> d) Details of the notifications to parents and guardians on every admission, transfer or release of the juveniles in their care at the time of commitment;
>
> e) Details of known physical and mental health problems, including drug and alcohol abuse.

The above-mentioned information should be provided without delay to the parents and guardians or closest relative of the juvenile.

On admission, juveniles will be given a copy of rules governing the facility and a written description of their rights and obligations in a language they can understand, together with the address of the authorities competent to receive complaints and the address of agencies which provide legal assistance. For those who are illiterate or cannot understand the language in the written form, the information shall be conveyed in a comprehensible manner.

Classification and placement

As soon as possible after admission, each juvenile should be interviewed and a psychological and social report identifying factors relevant to the care and programme required by the juvenile should be prepared. This report, together with that of a medical officer who has examined the juvenile upon admission, should be forwarded to the director for the purpose of determining the most appropriate placement of the juvenile within the facility. When special rehabilitative treatment is required, and the length of the stay permits, trained personnel should prepare a written, individualized treatment plan specifying objectives, time-frame, means, stages and potential delays.

Detention of juveniles should take place only under conditions taking account of their particular needs, status, age, personality, sex and type of offence, to ensure their protection from harmful influences and risk situations. The principal criterion for the separation of different categories of juveniles should be the type of care best suited to individual needs.

In all detention facilities, juveniles should be separated from adults, unless they are members of the same family. Under controlled conditions, juveniles may be brought together with carefully selected adults as part of a special programme shown to be beneficial for the juveniles concerned.

Open detention facilities—those with no or minimal security measures—for juveniles should be established. The population in such facilities should be as small as possible. The number of juveniles detained in closed facilities should be small enough to enable individualized treatment. Detention facilities should be decentralized and of such size as to facilitate contact with families. Small-scale facilities should be established and integrated into the social, economic and cultural environment of the community.

Physical environment and accommodation

Juveniles deprived of their liberty shall have the right to facilities and services meeting all requirements of health and human dignity.

Design of facilities should be in keeping with the rehabilitative aim, with due regard for privacy, sensory stimuli, opportunities for association between peers, sports and physical exercise and leisure activities. Risk of fire should be minimized and safe evacuation ensured. Facilities should not be located where there are known health or other hazards.

Sleeping accommodation should consist of small group dormitories or individual bedrooms, while bearing in mind local standards. During sleeping hours, there should be regular, unobtrusive supervision. Every juvenile should, in accord with local or national standards, be provided with separate and sufficient bedding, clean when issued and changed often enough to ensure cleanliness.

Sanitary installations should be so located and of a sufficient standard to enable every juvenile to comply with physical needs in privacy and in a clean and decent manner.

The possession of personal effects is a basic element of the right to privacy and essential to psychological well-being. The right to possess and store personal effects is to be fully respected. Those effects the juvenile does not choose to retain or that are confiscated should be placed in safe custody, and an inventory thereof signed by the juvenile. All such articles and money should be returned to the juvenile on release, except in so far as he or she has been authorized to spend money or send such property out of the facility. If a juvenile receives or is found in possession of medicine, the medical officer is to decide what use to make of it.

To the extent possible, juveniles should have the right to use their own clothing. Facilities should ensure that each juvenile has personal clothing suitable for the climate and adequate to ensure good health, and which in no manner shall be degrading or humiliating. Juveniles removed from or leaving a facility should be allowed to wear their own clothing.

Every detention facility shall ensure suitably prepared food presented at normal mealtimes and of a quality and quantity to meet dietary, hygienic and health standards and, as far as possible, religious or cultural requirements. Clean drinking water is to be available at any time.

Education, vocational training and work

Every juvenile of compulsory school age has the right to education suited to his or her needs and designed to prepare him or her for return to society. Such education should be provided outside the facility in community schools wherever possible. Special attention should be given to the education of juveniles of foreign origin or with particular cultural or ethnic needs and those who are illiterate or have cognitive difficulties have a right to special education.

Juveniles above compulsory school age who wish to continue their education should be permitted and encouraged to do so.

Diplomas or educational certificates awarded to juveniles while in detention shoud not indicate in any way that the juvenile has been institutionalized.

Every facility should provide access to a library adequately stocked with instructional and recreational books.

Every juvenile has the right to receive vocational training.

With due regard to proper vocational selection and the requirements of institutional administration, juveniles should be able to choose the type of work they wish to perform.

All protective national and international standards applicable to child labour should apply to juveniles deprived of their liberty.

Wherever possible, juveniles should be provided with opportunities to perform remunerated labour, if possible within the local community, as a complement to the vocational training provided. The organization and methods of work offered in detention facilities should resemble as closely as possible those of similar work in the community.

Every juvenile who performs work has the right to equitable remuneration. Interests of juveniles and their vocational training should not be subordinated to the purpose of making a profit for the detention facility or a third party. Part of the earnings of the juvenile normally should be set aside for a savings fund to be handed over at release. The juvenile has the right to the remainder, to purchase personal articles, indemnify the victim of his or her offence or send to his or her family or other persons outside the detention facility.

Recreation

Every juvenile has the right to a suitable amount of time for daily free exercise, in the open air when weather permits, during which recreational and physical training normally should be provided. Adequate space, installations and equipment are to be provided. There should be additional time for daily leisure activities, including arts and crafts skill development if the juvenile so wishes. Remedial physical education and therapy under medical supervision should be offered to juveniles needing it.

Religion

Every juvenile is to be allowed to satisfy the needs of his or her religious or spiritual life, by attending services in the facility or by conducting his or her own services and having possession of necessary books or items of religious observance and instruction. If a facility contains a sufficient number of juveniles of a given religion, one or more qualified representatives of that religion should be appointed to hold regular services and pay pastoral visits. Every juvenile has the right to visits from qualified representatives of any religion of his or her choice, as well as the right not to participate in religious services and freely to decline religious education, counselling or indoctrination.

Medical care

Every juvenile shall receive adequate medical care, both preventive and remedial, including dental, ophthalmological and mental health care, as well as pharmaceutical products and special diets as medically indicated. All care should, where possible, be provided to detained juveniles through the appropriate facilities of the community in which the detention facility is located, to prevent stigmatization and promote integration into the community.

Every juvenile has a right to examination by a physician immediately upon admission to a detention facility, for the purpose of recording evidence of prior ill-treatment and identifying any physical or mental condition requiring treatment.

The medical service should seek to detect and treat any physical or mental illness, substance abuse or other condition that may hinder the integration of the juvenile into society. Every facility should have immediate access to adequate medical facilities and equipment appropriate to the number and requirements of its residents and to staff trained in preventive care and emergency treatment. Every juvenile who complains of or demonstrates symptoms of physical or mental difficulties should be examined promptly by a medical officer.

Any medical officer who believes the physical or mental health of a juvenile has been or will be injuriously affected by continued detention, a hunger strike or any condition of detention should report this fact immediately to the director of the facility and to the independent authority responsible for safeguarding the well-being of the juvenile.

A juvenile suffering from mental illness should be treated in a specialized institution under independent medical management. Steps should be taken to continue mental health care after release.

Juvenile detention facilities should adopt specialized drug abuse prevention and rehabilitation programmes administered by qualified personnel and adapted to the age, sex and other requirements of the juveniles concerned. Detoxification facilities and services staffed by trained personnel should be available.

Medicines should be administered only for necessary treatment and, when possible, after having obtained the informed consent of the juvenile concerned. In particular, they must not be administered to elicit information or a confession, as a punishment or as a means of restraint. Juveniles shall never be testees in the experimental use of drugs and treatment. Administration of any drug should always be authorized and carried out by qualified medical personnel.

Notification of illness, injury and death

The family or guardian of a juvenile and any other person designated by the juvenile have the right to be informed of the state of health of the juvenile on request and in the event of any important changes in the health of the juvenile. Any parent, guardian or designated person shall be notified immediately in case of death, illness requiring transfer to an outside medical facility or a condition requiring clinical care within the detention facility for more than 48 hours. Notification should be given to the consular authorities of the State of which a foreign juvenile is a citizen.

Upon the death of a juvenile during the period of deprivation of liberty, the nearest relative has the right to inspect the death certificate, see the body and determine the method of its disposal. There should be an independent inquiry into the causes of death, the report of which should be made accessible to the nearest relative. This inquiry should also be made when the death occurs within six months of the date of the juvenile's release and there is reason to believe that the death is related to the period of detention.

A juvenile should be informed at the earliest possible time of the death or serious illness or injury of any immediate family member and have the opportunity to attend the funeral or go to the bedside of a critically ill relative.

Contacts with the wider community

Juveniles should have adequate communication with the outside world, which is part of fair and humane treatment and essential to preparation for return to society. Communication should be allowed with families, friends and other persons or representatives of reputable outside organizations. Juveniles should be allowed to leave the facility for a visit to home and family and should receive special permission to leave for educational or vocational reasons. Should the juvenile be serving a sentence, time spent outside a facility should be counted as part of the period of sentence.Every juvenile has the right to receive regular and frequent visits, in principle once a week and not less than once a month, in privacy and with unrestricted communication with family and the defence counsel.

Every juvenile has the right to communicate in writing or by telephone at least twice a week with the person of his or her choice, unless legally restricted, and should be assisted in enjoying this right. Every juvenile has the right to receive correspondence.

Juveniles have the right to keep informed of the news through newspapers and periodicals, access to radio, television and motion pictures, and visits of the representatives of any lawful club or organization.

Limitations of physical restraint and the use of force

Recourse to instruments of restraint and to force should be prohibited, except as set forth below.

Instruments of restraint and force can be used only in exceptional cases, where all other control methods have failed, and only as authorized by law and regulation. They should not cause humiliation or degradation, and should be used restrictively and only for the shortest possible time. By order of the director of the administration, such instruments might be resorted to in order to prevent the juvenile from inflicting self-injury, injuries to others or serious destruction of property. In such instances, the director should consult medical and other relevant personnel at once and report to the higher administrative authority.

The carrying and use of weapons by personnel should be prohibited in any facilities where juveniles are detained.

Disciplinary procedures

Disciplinary measures should promote safety and an ordered community and should be consistent with upholding the dignity of the juvenile and instilling a sense of justice, self-respect and respect for the rights of others.

All cruel, inhumane or degrading disciplinary measures shall be strictly prohibited, including corporal punishment, placement in a dark cell and solitary confinement. Reduction of diet and denial of contact with family members should be prohibited. Labour should always be viewed as an educational tool and a means of promoting the self-respect of the juvenile and should not be imposed as a disciplinary measure. No juvenile should be sanctioned more than once for the same infraction. Collective sanctions should be prohibited.

Legislation or regulations should be established concerning the following:

a) Conduct constituting a disciplinary offence;

b) Type and duration of disciplinary sanctions that may be inflicted;

c) The authority competent to impose such sanctions;

d) The authority competent to consider appeals.

A report of misconduct should be presented promptly to the proper authority, and decided on without undue delay. A thorough examination of the case should be conducted.

No juvenile should be sanctioned except in accord with the law and regulations in force. No juvenile should be sanctioned without being informed of the alleged infraction and given a proper opportunity to present a defence, including right of appeal to a competent impartial authority. Complete records should be kept of all disciplinary proceedings.

No juveniles should be responsible for disciplinary functions except in the supervision of specified social, educational or sports activities or in self-government programmes.

Inspection and complaints

Qualified inspectors or an equivalent authority not belonging to the administration of the facility should conduct inspections on a regular basis and undertake unannounced inspections on their own initiative and should enjoy full guarantees of independence. Inspectors should have unrestricted access to all persons employed by or working in any facility where juveniles are or may be deprived of their liberty and to all juveniles and all records of such facilities.

Qualified medical officers attached to the inspecting authority or the public health service should participate in inspections, evaluating compliance with rules concerning physical environment, hygiene, accommodation, food, exercise and medical services. Every juvenile has the right to talk in confidence to any inspecting officer.

After completing the inspection, the inspector should submit a report including an evaluation of compliance with the present Rules and relevant national law and recommendations for ensuring compliance. Any facts indicating violation of legal provisions should be communicated to competent authorities for investigation and prosecution.

Every juvenile should be able to make requests or complaints to the director of the facility or his or her authorized representative, or to the central administration, the judicial authority or other proper authorities through the proper channels, without censorship as to substance, and should be informed of the response without delay.

Efforts should be made to establish an independent office (ombusdman) to investigate complaints made by juveniles deprived of their liberty and achieve equitable settlements.

Juveniles have the right to request assistance from family members, legal counsellors, humanitarian groups or others to make a complaint. Illiterate juveniles should be assisted if they need to use the services of agencies providing legal counsel or which are competent to receive complaints.

Return to the community

Procedures, including early release, should be designed to assist juveniles returning to society, family life, education or employment after release.

Services to assist juveniles in re-establishing themselves in society should ensure, to the extent possible, suitable residence, employment, clothing and sufficient means. Representatives of agencies providing such services should be consulted and should have access to juveniles while detained.

Personnel

Personnel should be qualified and include a sufficient number of educators, vocational instructors, counsellors, social workers, psychiatrists and psychologists, normally employed on a full-time basis, but not excluding part-time or volunteer workers as appropriate.

The administration should carefully select and recruit every grade and type of personnel, provide adequate remuneration and encourage conduct that will deserve and gain the respect of juveniles.

Organization and management should facilitate communications between different categories of staff and between staff and administration.

Personnel are to be trained in child psychology, child welfare and international standards and norms of human rights and the rights of the child, including the present Rules, and to receive in-service training in professional skills.

The director of a facility should be qualified by administrative ability, suitable training and experience and should work full-time.

Personnel should respect and protect human dignity and fundamental rights. In particular:

> a) No staff member may inflict, instigate or tolerate any act of torture or any harsh, cruel, inhuman or degrading treatment under any pretext;
>
> b) All personnel should rigorously oppose corruption and report incidents without delay to the competent authorities;
>
> c) All personnel should respect the present Rules and report any serious violation;
>
> d) All personnel should ensure full protection of the physical and mental health of juveniles, including protection from physical, sexual and emotional abuse and exploitation;
>
> e) All personnel should respect the right of the juvenile to privacy, and should safeguard all confidential matters concerning juveniles and their families learned as a result of their professional capacity;

f) All personnel should seek to minimize any
differences between life inside and outside the
detention facility which tend to lessen due respect
to the dignity of juveniles as human beings.

Basic Principles on the Use of Force and Firearms by Law Enforcement Officials

Adopted by the Eighth Crime Congress

General provisions

Governments and law enforcement agencies shall adopt and
implement rules and regulations on the use of force and firearms
against persons by law enforcement officials and keep associated
ethical issues constantly under review.

Governments and law enforcement agencies should develop a
range of means as broad as possible and equip law enforcement
officials with various types of weapons and ammunition allowing
for differentiated use of force and firearms, to include non-lethal
incapacitating weapons, with a view to increasingly restraining
applications of means causing death or injury.

Development and deployment of non-lethal incapacitating
weapons should be carefully evaluated to minimize the risk of
endangering uninvolved persons, and use should be carefully
controlled.

In carrying out their duty, law enforcement officials shall as far as
possible apply non-violent means before resorting to force and
firearms. They may use force and firearms only if other means
remain ineffective or without any promise of achieving the
intended result.

Whenever lawful use of force and firearms is unavoidable, law
enforcement officials shall:

a) Exercise restraint and act in proportion to
the seriousness of the offence and the
legitimate objective;

b) Minimize damage and injury, and respect
and preserve human life;

c) Ensure that assistance and medical aid are
rendered to any injured or affected persons at
the earliest possible moment;

d) Ensure that relatives or close friends of the
injured or affected person are notified at
the earliest moment.

Where injury or death is caused by the use of force and firearms by law enforcement officials, they shall report the incident promptly to their superior.

Governments shall ensure that arbitrary or abusive use of force and firearms by law enforcement officials is punished as a criminal offence under their law.

Exceptional circumstances, such as internal political instability or any other public emergency, may not be invoked to justify any departure from these basic principles.

Special provisions

Law enforcement officials shall not use firearms against persons except in self-defence or defence of others against the imminent threat of death or serious injury, to prevent the perpetration of a particularly serious crime involving grave threat to life, to arrest a person presenting such a danger and resisting their authority, or to prevent his or her escape, and only when less extreme means are insufficient to achieve these objectives.

In the circumstances provided for under the above principle, law enforcement officials shall identify themselves as such and give a clear warning of their intent to use firearms, with sufficient time for the warning to be observed, unless to do so would unduly place the law enforcement officials at risk or would create a risk of death or serious harm to other persons, or would be clearly inappropriate or pointless in the circumstances of the incident.

Rules and regulations should include guidelines that:

a) Specify the circumstances under which law
enforcement officials are authorized to carry
firearms and prescribe the types of firearms and
ammunition permitted;

b) Ensure that firearms are used only in appropriate circumstances and in a manner likely to decrease the risk of unnecessary harm;

c) Prohibit the use of firearms and ammunition that cause unwarranted injury or present an unwarranted risk;

d) Regulate the control, storage and issuing of firearms, including procedures for ensuring that law enforcement officials are accountable for the firearms and ammunition issued to them;

e) Provide for warnings to be given, if appropriate, when firearms are to be discharged;

f) Provide for a system of reporting whenever law enforcement officials use firearms in the performance of their duty.

Policing unlawful assemblies

As everyone is allowed to participate in lawful and peaceful assemblies, Governments and law enforcement agencies and officials shall recognize that force and firearms may be used only in accord with the following two principles:

a) In the dispersal of assemblies that are unlawful but non-violent, law enforcement officials shall avoid the use of force or, where that is not practicable, shall restrict force used to the minimum necessary;

b) In the dispersal of violent assemblies, firearms may be used only when less dangerous means are not practicable and only to the minimum extent necessary.

Policing persons in custody or detention

Law enforcement officials shall not use force in relations with persons in custody or detention except when strictly necessary for the maintenance of security and order within the institution, or when personal safety is threatened.

They shall not use firearms in such relations except in self-defence or in the defence of others against the immediate threat of death or serious injury, or when strictly necessary to prevent the escape of a person in custody or detention who presents an imminent threat.

Qualifications, training and counselling

All law enforcement officials are to be selected by proper screening procedures, have appropriate moral, psychological and physical qualities for effective exercise of their functions and receive continuous professional training. Their continued fitness to perform should be subject to periodic review.

Law enforcement officials are to be trained and tested in accord with appropriate proficiency standards in the use of force. Those required to carry firearms should be authorized to do so only upon completion of special training in their use.

Questions of police ethics and human rights shall be given special attention in the training of law enforcement officials, including the peaceful settlement of conflicts, the understanding of crowd behaviour, and methods of persuasion, negotiation and mediation. Law enforcement agencies should review their training programmes and operational procedures in the light of particular incidents.

Stress counselling should be made available to law enforcement officials who are involved in situations where force and firearms are used.

Reporting and review procedures

Effective reporting and review procedures are to be established for all incidents where use of force or firearms causes injury or death or when firearms are used in the performance of law enforcement. An effective review process is to be available and independent administrative or prosecutorial authorities are to be in a position to exercise jurisdiction in appropriate circumstances. In cases of death and serious injury or other grave consequences, a detailed report shall be sent promptly to the competent authorities.

Persons affected by the use of force and firearms or their legal representatives shall have access to an independent process, including a judicial process. In the event of the death of such persons, this provision shall apply to their dependants.

Superior officers are to be held responsible if they know, or should have known, that law enforcement officials under their command are resorting, or have resorted, to unlawful use of force and firearms, and they did not take all measures in their power to prevent, suppress or report such use.

No criminal or disciplinary sanction is to be imposed on law enforcement officials who, in compliance with the Code of Conduct for Law Enforcement Officials and these basic principles, refuse to carry out an order to use force or firearms, or who report such use by other officials.

Obedience to superior orders shall be no defence if law enforcement officials knew that an order to use force and firearms resulting in the death or serious injury of a person was manifestly unlawful and had a reasonable opportunity to refuse to follow it. In any case, responsibility also rests on the superiors who gave the unlawful orders.

Basic Principles on the Role of Lawyers
Adopted by the Eighth Crime Congress

Access to lawyers and legal services

All persons are entitled to call upon the assistance of a lawyer of their choice to protect and establish their rights and defend them in all stages of criminal proceedings.

Governments shall ensure that efficient procedures and responsive mechanisms for effective and equal access to lawyers are provided for all persons within their territory and subject to their jurisdiction, without distinction or discrimination of any kind.

Governments shall ensure sufficient funding and other resources for legal services to the poor and, as necessary, other disadvantaged persons. Professional associations of lawyers shall cooperate to this end.

Programmes to inform the public about their rights and duties under the law and the important role of lawyers in protecting fundamental freedoms are to be promoted. Special attention should be given to the poor and disadvantaged to enable them to assert their rights and where necessary call upon the assistance of lawyers.

Special safeguards in criminal justice matters

All persons are to be informed immediately by a competent authority of their right to be assisted by a lawyer of their own choice upon arrest or detention or when charged with a criminal offence.

All persons are entitled to have a lawyer of experience and competence commensurate with the nature of the offence assigned to them without payment if they lack sufficient means.

All persons arrested or detained shall have prompt access to a lawyer, and in any case within 48 hours.

All arrested, detained or imprisoned persons shall be provided with adequate opportunities, time and facilities to be visited by and to communicate and consult with a lawyer, without delay, interception or censorship and in full confidentiality. Such consultations may be within sight, but not within hearing, of law enforcement officials.

Qualifications and training

Lawyers are to have appropriate education and training and be made aware of the ideals and ethical duties of the lawyer and of human rights and fundamental freedoms recognized by national and international law.

There is to be no discrimination of any kind against a person with respect to entry into or continued practice within the legal profession, except that a requirement that a lawyer must be a national of the country concerned shall not be considered discriminatory.

In countries where there exist groups, communities or regions whose needs for legal services are not met, particularly where such groups have distinct cultures, traditions or languages or have been the victims of past discrimination, special measures should be taken to provide opportunities for candidates from these groups to enter the legal profession and receive training appropriate to the needs of their groups.

Duties and responsibilities

Lawyers shall at all times maintain the honour and dignity of their profession as essential agents of the administration of justice.

The duties of lawyers towards their clients shall include:

> a) Advising clients as to their legal rights and obligations, and to the working of the legal system in so far as it is relevant to the rights and obligations of their clients;
>
> b) Assisting clients in every appropriate way, and taking legal action to protect their interests;
>
> c) Assisting clients before courts, tribunals or administrative authorities, where appropriate.

Lawyers shall seek to uphold human rights and fundamental freedoms recognized by national and international law and at all times act freely and diligently in accord with the law and recognized standards of the legal profession.

Lawyers shall always loyally respect the interests of their clients.

Guarantees for the functioning of lawyers

Where the security of lawyers is threatened as a result of discharging their functions, they shall be adequately safeguarded by the authorities.

Lawyers shall not be identified with their clients or their clients' causes as a result of discharging their functions.

No court or administrative authority before whom the right to counsel is recognized shall refuse to recognize the right of a lawyer to appear before it for his or her client unless that lawyer has been disqualified in accord with national law and practice.

Lawyers shall enjoy civil and penal immunity for relevant statements made in good faith in written or oral pleadings or in their professional appearances before a court, tribunal or other legal or administrative authority.

It is the duty of the competent authorities to ensure that lawyers have access to appropriate information, files and documents in their possession or control in time to enable lawyers to provide effective legal assistance to their clients and at the earliest appropriate time.

Governments shall recognize and respect that all communications and consultations between lawyers and their clients within their professional relationship are confidential.

Freedom of expression and association

Lawyers, like other citizens, are entitled to freedom of expression, belief, association and assembly. In particular, they shall have the right to take part in public discussion of matters concerning the law and human rights and to join or form local, national or international organizations and attend meetings, without suffering professional restrictions. In exercising these rights, lawyers shall always conduct themselves in accord with the law and recognized standards of the profession.

Professional associations of lawyers

Lawyers are entitled to form and join self-governing professional associations to represent their interests, promote continuing education and training and protect professional integrity. The executive body of the professional associations shall be elected by its members and exercise its functions without external interference.

Professional associations of lawyers shall cooperate with Governments to ensure effective and equal access to legal services for all and that lawyers are able, without improper interference, to counsel and assist their clients.

Disciplinary proceedings

Codes of professional conduct are to be established by the legal profession through appropriate organs, or by legislation, in accord with national law and custom and recognized international standards and norms.

Charges or complaints made against lawyers in their professional capacities shall be processed expeditiously and fairly under appropriate procedures. Lawyers have the right to a fair hearing, including the right to be assisted by a lawyer of their choice.

Disciplinary proceedings shall be determined in accord with the code of professional conduct and other recognized standards and ethics of the legal profession.

Guidelines on the Role of Prosecutors

Adopted by the Eighth Crime Congress

Qualifications, selection and training

Persons selected as prosecutors shall be individuals of integrity and ability, with appropriate training and qualifications. States shall ensure that:

> a) Selection criteria for prosecutors embody safeguards against appointments based on partiality or prejudice of any kind, save that it shall not be considered discriminatory to require a candidate to be a national of the country concerned;

> b) Prosecutors have appropriate education and training and are aware of the ideals and duties of their office, of constitutional and statutory protections for the rights of the suspect and the victim, and of human rights and fundamental freedoms recognized by national and international law.

Status and conditions of service

Prosecutors, as essential agents of the administration of justice, shall at all times maintain the honour and dignity of their profession.

States shall ensure that prosecutors can perform professional functions without intimidation, hindrance, harassment, improper interference or unjustified exposure to civil, penal or other liability.

Prosecutors and their families shall be physically protected by the authorities when personal safety is threatened due to discharge of professional functions.

Reasonable conditions of service of prosecutors, adequate remuneration and, where applicable, tenure, pension and age of retirement shall be set out by law or published rules or regulations.

Promotion of prosecutors, wherever such a system exists, shall be based on objective factors, such as ability, integrity and experience, and decided through fair and impartial procedures.

Freedom of expression and association

Prosecutors, like other citizens, are entitled to freedom of expression, belief, association and assembly. In particular, they shall have the right to take part in public discussion of matters concerning the law and human rights and to join or form local, national or international organizations and attend meetings, without suffering professional restrictions. In exercising these rights, prosecutors shall always conduct themselves in accord with the law and recognized standards of the profession.

Prosecutors are to be free to form and join professional associations or other organizations to represent their interests, promote professional training and protect their status.

Role in criminal proceedings

The office of prosecutors shall be strictly separated from judicial proceedings.

Prosecutors are to take an active role in criminal proceedings, including institution of prosecution and, where authorized by law or consistent with local practice, in the investigation of crime, supervision over the legality of these investigations, supervision of the execution of court decisions and the exercise of other functions as representatives of the public interest.

Prosecutors shall perform their duties fairly, consistently and expeditiously, and respect and protect human dignity and human rights.

In the performance of their duties, prosecutors shall:

> a) Carry out their functions impartially and avoid all kinds of discrimination;
>
> b) Protect the public interest, act with objectivity, take account of the position of the suspect and the victim and pay attention to all relevant circumstances, irrespective of whether they are to the advantage or disadvantage of the suspect;
>
> c) Keep matters in their possession confidential, unless performance of duty or needs of justice require otherwise;
>
> d) Consider the views and concerns of victims and ensure they are informed of their rights in accord with the Declaration of Basic Principles of Justice for Victims of Abuse of Power.

Prosecutors shall not initiate or continue prosecution, or shall make every effort to stay proceedings, when an impartial investigation shows the charge to be unfounded.

When prosecutors come into possession of evidence against suspects that they know or believe to be obtained through recourse to unlawful methods, especially involving torture or cruel, inhuman or degrading treatment or punishment, or other abuses of human rights, they shall refuse to use such evidence against anyone other than those who used such methods, or inform the court accordingly, and shall take all necessary steps to ensure that those responsible are brought to justice.

Discretionary functions

In countries where prosecutors are vested with discretionary functions, the law or published rules or regulations shall provide guidelines to enhance fairness and consistency in taking decisions, including institution or waiver of prosecution.

Alternatives to prosecution

In accord with national law, prosecutors should consider waiving prosecution, discontinuing proceedings conditionally or unconditionally or diverting criminal cases from the formal justice system, with full respect for the rights of suspect and victim. States should fully explore the possibility of adopting diversion schemes.

In countries where prosecutors are vested with discretion in deciding whether or not to prosecute a juvenile, special consideration should be given to the nature and gravity of the offence, protection of society and the personality and background of the juvenile. They shall particularly consider available alternatives to prosecution, and take prosecutory action only to the extent strictly necessary.

Relations with other government agencies or institutions

To ensure fairness and effectiveness, prosecutors shall cooperate with the police, the courts, the legal profession, public defenders and other government agencies or institutions.

Disciplinary proceedings

Disciplinary offences of prosecutors shall be based on law or lawful regulations. Complaints which allege that prosecutors acted in a manner out of the range of professional standards shall be processed expeditiously and fairly under appropriate procedures. Prosecutors have the right to a fair hearing. The decision is to be subject to independent review.

Disciplinary proceedings against prosecutors shall guarantee an objective evaluation and decision and be determined in accord with the law, the code of professional conduct and other established standards and in the light of the present Guidelines.

Observance of the Guidelines

Prosecutors shall respect the present Guidelines and to the best of their capability prevent and oppose any violations thereof.

Prosecutors with reason to believe a violation of the Guidelines has occurred or is about to occur shall report the matter to their superior authorities and, where necessary, to other appropriate authorities vested with reviewing or remedial power.

Model Treaty on Extradition
Adopted by the Eighth Crime Congress

Article 1
Obligation to extradite

Each Party agrees to extradite to the other any person who is wanted in the requesting State for prosecution for an extraditable offence or for the imposition or enforcement of a sentence in respect of such an offence.

Article 2
Extraditable offences

Extraditable offences are those punishable under the laws of both Parties by imprisonment or deprivation of liberty for a maximum period of at least [one/two] year(s), or by a more severe penalty.

Where request for extradition relates to a person wanted for enforcement of a sentence, extradition shall be granted only if a period of at least [four/six] months remains to be served.

In determining whether or an offence is punishable under the laws of both Parties, it shall not matter whether:

> a) The laws of both Parties place the acts or omissions constituting the offence within the same category of offence or denominate the offence by the same terminology;

> b) Under the laws of the Parties, the constituent elements of the offence differ; it is the totality of the acts or omissions that shall be taken into account.

Where extradition is sought for an offence against a law relating to taxation, customs duties or other revenue matters, extradition may not be refused on the ground that the law of the requesting State does not impose the same kind of tax or duty.

If the request for extradition includes several separate offences each of which is punishable under the laws of both Parties, but some of which do not fulfil other conditions set out in paragraph 1 of this article, the requested Party may grant extradition for the latter offences provided the persons is to be extradited for at least one extraditable offence.

Article 3
Mandatory grounds for refusal

Extradition shall not be granted in any of the following circumstances:

> a) If the offence for which extradition is requested is regarded as a political offence;

> b) If there are grounds to believe the request has been made to prosecute or punish a person on account of that person's race, religion, nationality, ethnic origin, political opinions, sex or status, or that the person's position may be prejudiced for any of these reasons;

> c) If the offence is an offence under military law and not also an offence under criminal law;

> d) If final judgement has been rendered against the person in the requested State in respect of the offence for which the persons' extradition is requested;

e) If the person whose extradition has been requested has, under the law of either Party, become immune from prosecution or punishment for any reason, including lapse of time or amnesty;

f) If the person would be subjected to torture or cruel, inhuman treatment or degrading punishment or if that person has not or would not receive the minimum guarantees in criminal proceedings as contained in the International Covenant on Civil and Political Rights, article 14.

g) If the judgement of the requesting State has been rendered *in absentia*, the convicted person has not had sufficient notice of the trial nor opportunity to arrange for a defence and has not or will not have the opportunity to have the case retried.

Article 4
Optional grounds for refusal

Extradition may be refused in any of the following circumstances:

a) If the person whose extradition is requested is a national of the requested State;

b) If the competent authorities of the requested State have decided either not to institute or to terminate proceedings against the person for the offence for which extradition is requested;

c) If prosecution in the requested State is pending for the same offence;

d) If the offence carries the death penalty under the law of the requesting State;

e) If the offence has been committed outside the territory of either Party and the law of the requested State does not provide for jurisdiction over such an offence committed outside its territory;

f) If the offence is regarded under the law of the requested State as having been committed in whole or in part within that State;

g) If the person whose extradition has been requested has been sentenced or would be liable to be tried in the requesting State by an extraordinary or ad hoc court or tribunal;

h) If extradition would be incompatible with humanitarian considerations in view of age, health or other personal circumstances of that person.

Article 5
Channels of communication and required documents

A request for extradition shall be made in writing and transmitted, along with supporting documents, through diplomatic channels directly between the ministries of justice or other designated authorities.

A request shall be accompanied by the following:

a) In all cases,

i) As accurate a description as possible of the person sought and information to help establish that person's identity, nationality and location;

ii) The text of the relevant provision of the law creating the offence and a statement of the penalty that can be imposed;

b) If a warrant for arrest has been issued, by a certified copy of that warrant, a statement of the offence for which extradition is requested and a description of the acts or omissions constituting the alleged offence;

c) If the person has been convicted, by a statement of the offence and a description of the acts or omissions constituting the offence and by the original or certified copy of the judgement;

d) If the person has been convicted in his or her absence, in addition to the documents set out in paragraph (c), by a statement as to the legal means available to the person to prepare a defence or have the case retried;

e) If the person has been convicted but no sentence imposed, by a statement of the offence, a document setting out the conviction and a statement affirming intent to impose a sentence.

The documents shall be accompanied by a translation into the language of the requested State or another language acceptable to that State.

Article 6
Simplified extradition procedure

The requested State may grant extradition after receipt of a request for provisional arrest, provided that the person sought explicitly consents before a competent authority.

Article 7
Certification and authentication

Except as provided by this Treaty, a request for extradition and the supporting documents thereto shall not require certification or authentication.

Article 8
Additional information

If the requested State considers that the information provided in a request for extradition is not sufficient, it may request additional information to be furnished within such reasonable time as it specifies.

Article 9
Provisional arrest

In case of urgency, the requesting State may apply for the provisional arrest of the person sought pending presentation of the request for extradition.

The application for provisional arrest shall contain a description of the person sought, a statement of the existence of one of the documents mentioned in paragraph 2 of article 5, a statement of the punishment that has or can be imposed and a concise statement of the facts of the case and the location, where known, of the person.

The requested State shall decide on the application and communicate its decision without delay.

The person arrested shall be set at liberty upon the expiration of (40) days if a request for extradition supported by the relevant documents has not been received.

Such release shall not prevent rearrest and institution of extradition proceedings if the request is subsequently received.

Article 10
Decision on the request

The requested State shall promptly communicate its decision on the request for extradition to the requesting State.

Reasons shall be given for any complete or partial refusal of the request.

Article 11
Surrender of the person

Upon being informed that extradition has been granted, the Parties shall without undue delay arrange for the surrender of the person sought and the requested State shall inform the requesting State of the length of time for which the person was detained with a view to surrender.

The person shall be removed from the territory of the requested State within such reasonable time as the requested State specifies and, if the person is not removed by then, the requested State may release the person and may refuse extradition for the same offence.

If circumstances beyond its control prevent a Party from surrendering or removing the person to be extradited, it shall notify the other Party and a new date of surrender will be agreed upon.

Article 12
Postponed or conditional surrender

The requested State may postpone the surrender of a person sought in order to proceed against that person or enforce a sentence imposed for an offence other than that for which extradition is sought.

The requested State may, instead of postponing surrender, temporarily surrender the person sought to the requesting State in accord with conditions determined between the Parties.

Article 13
Surrender of property

To the extent permitted under the law of the requested State and subject to the rights of third parties, all property found in the requested State that has been acquired as a result of the offence or that may be required as evidence shall, upon request, be surrendered if extradition is granted.

Said property may, on request, be surrendered to the requesting State even if the extradition having been agreed to cannot be carried out.

When said property is liable to seizure or confiscation in the requested State, it may retain it or temporarily hand it over.

Where the law of the requested State or protection of the rights of third parties so require, any property so surrendered shall be returned to the requested State free of charge after completion of proceedings, if that State so requests.

Article 14
Rule of speciality

A person extradited under this Treaty shall not be proceeded against, sentenced, detained, re-extradited to a third State, or subjected to any other restriction of personal liberty in the territory of the requesting State for any offence committed before surrender other than:

> a) An offence for which extradition was granted;

> b) Any other offence in respect of which the requested State consents.

A request for the consent of the requested State under this article shall be accompanied by the documents mentioned in paragaph 2 of article 5 and a legal record of any statement made by the extradited person with respect to the offence.

Paragraph 1 of this article shall not apply if the person has had an opportunity to leave the requesting State and has not done so within [30/45] days of final discharge in respect of the offence for which that person was extradited or if the person has voluntarily returned to the territory of the requesting State after leaving it.

Article 15
Transit

Where a person is to be extradited to a Party from a third State through the territory of the other Party, the Party to which the person is to be extradited shall request the other Party to permit transit through its territory.

The requested State shall grant such a request expeditiously unless its essential interests would be prejudiced thereby.

The State of transit shall ensure legal provisions enabling the person to be held in custody during transit.

In the event of an unscheduled landing, the Party to be requested to permit transit may, at the request of the escorting officer, hold the person in custody for [48 hours] pending receipt of the transit request.

Article 16
Concurrent requests

If a party receives requests for extradition for the same person from both the other Party and a third State it shall, at its discretion, determine to which of those States the person is to be extradited.

Article 17
Costs

The requested State shall meet the cost of any proceedings in its jurisdiction arising out of a request for extradition.

The requested State shall also bear the costs incurred in its territory with the seizure and handing over of property or the arrest and detention of the person sought.

The requesting State shall bear the costs incurred in conveying the person from the territory of the requested State, including transit costs.

Article 18
Final provisions

This Treaty is subject to (ratification, acceptance or approval).

This Treaty shall enter into force on the thirtieth day after the day on which the instruments of (ratification, acceptance or approval) are exchanged.

This Treaty shall apply to requests made after its entry into force, even if the relevant acts or omissions occurred prior to that date.

Either Party may denounce this Treaty by giving notice in writing to the other Party. Such denunciation shall take effect six months following the date on which notice is received by the other Party.

Model Treaty on Mutual Assistance in Criminal Matters

Adopted by the General Assembly as resolution 45/116 on the recommendation of the Eighth Congress

Article 1
Scope of application

The Parties shall afford to each other the widest possible measure of mutual assistance in investigations or court proceedings in respect of offences the punishment of which at the time of the request for assistance, falls within the jurisdiction of the judicial authorities of the Requesting State.

Mutual assistance to be afforded in accord with this Treaty may include:

a) Taking evidence or statements from persons;

b) Assisting in the availability of detained persons or others to give evidence or assist in investigations;

c) Effecting service of judicial documents;

d) Executing searches and seizures;

e) Examining objects and sites;

f) Providing information and evidentiary items;

g) Providing relevant documents and records.

This Treaty does not apply to:

a) The arrest or detention of any person with a view to extradition;

b) The enforcement of criminal judgements imposed in the Requesting State except as permitted by law in the Requested State;

c) The transfer of persons in custody to serve sentences;

d) The transfer of proceedings in criminal matters.

Article 2
Other arrangements

Unless the Parties decide otherwise, this Treaty shall not affect obligations subsisting between them.

Article 3
Designation of competent authorities

Each Party shall designate and indicate to the other Party an authority or authorities through which requests for the purposes of this Treaty should be made.

Article 4
Refusal of assistance

Assistance may be refused if:

a) The Requested State is of the opinion that the request, if granted, would prejudice its sovereignty, security, public order or other essential public interests;

b) The offence is regarded as being of a political nature;

c) There are grounds to believe the request has been made for the purpose of prosecuting a person on account of race, sex, religion, nationality, ethnic origin or political opinions or that person's position may be prejudiced for any of those reasons;

d) The request relates to an offence subject to investigation or prosecution in the Requested State or which would be incompatible with this State's law on double jeopardy;

e) The Requested State is required to carry out compulsory measures inconsistent with its law and practice;

f) The act is an offence under military law, and not also an offence under ordinary criminal law.

Before refusing a request, the Requested State shall consider whether assistance may be granted subject to certain conditions. If the Requesting State accepts assistance under these conditions, it shall comply with them.

Reasons shall be given for any refusal or postponement of mutual assistance.

Article 5
Contents of requests

Requests for assistance shall include:

> a) The name of the requesting office and the competent authority conducting the investigation or court proceedings;

> b) The purpose of the request and a brief description of the assistance sought;

> c) A description of the facts alleged to constitute the offence and a statement of the relevant laws;

> d) The name and address of the person to be served, where necessary;

> e) The reasons for and details of any procedure or requirement that the Requesting State wishes to be followed;

> f) Specification of any time-limit to be complied with;

> g) Other necessary information.

Requests and supporting documents shall be accompanied by a translation into the language of the Requested State or another language acceptable to that State.

The Requested State may request additional information.

Article 6
Execution of requests

Requests for assistance shall be carried out promptly. To the extent consistent with the law of the Requested State, it shall carry out the request in the manner specified by the Requesting State.

Article 7
Return of material to the Requested State

Any property, records or documents handed over to the Requesting State shall be returned as soon as possible unless right of return is waived.

Article 8
Limitation on use

The Requesting State shall not use information provided for proceedings other than those stated in the request.

Article 9
Protection of confidentiality

Upon request:

> a) The Requested State shall endeavour to keep confidential the request for assistance and its contents;
>
> b) The Requesting State shall keep confidential evidence and information provided, except as needed for investigation and proceedings described in the request.

Article 10
Service of documents

The Requested State shall effect service of documents that are transmitted to it.

A request to effect service of summonses shall be made not less than...days before the date on which the appearance of a person is required. In urgent cases, the time requirement may be waived.

Article 11
Obtaining evidence

The Requested State shall take sworn or affirmed testimony for transmission to the Requesting State.

Upon request, the parties to the relevant proceedings in the Requesting State, their legal representatives and representatives of the Requesting State may be present at these proceedings.

Article 12
Right or obligation to decline to give evidence

A person required to give evidence may decline to do so where either:

> a) The law of the Requested State permits or requires that person to decline to give evidence in similar circumstances; or

b) The law of the Requesting State permits or requires that person to decline to give evidence in similar circumstances.

If a person claims a right or obligation to decline to give evidence under the law of the other State, a certificate of the competent authority of that other State as to the existence or non-existence of that right or obligation shall be relied on.

Article 13
Availability of persons in custody to give evidence or to assist in investigations

Upon request, and if the Requested State agrees and its law permits, a person in custody may, subject to his or her consent, be temporarily transferred to the Requesting State to give evidence or assist in the investigations.

The Requesting State shall hold that person in custody and shall return him or her at the conclusion of the matter under investigation or at such earlier time as that person's presence is no longer required.

Where the Requested State advises the Requesting State that the transferred person is no longer required to be held in custody, that person shall be set at liberty.

Article 14
Availability of other persons to give evidence or assist in investigations

The Requesting State may request the assistance of the Requested State in inviting a person:

a) To appear in proceedings in relation to a criminal matter, unless that person is the person charged; or

b) To assist in the investigations in relation to a criminal matter.

The Requested State shall invite the person to appear as a witness or expert in proceedings or to assist in investigations.

The request or the summons shall indicate the approximate allowances and the travel and subsistence expenses payable by the Requesting State.

Upon request, the Requested State may grant the person an advance, to be refunded by the Requesting State.

Article 15
Safe conduct

Where a person is in the Requesting State pursuant to a request for assistance:

> a) That person shall not be detained, prosecuted, punished or subjected to any other restrictions of personal liberty in respect of any acts or omissions that preceded the person's departure from the Requested State;
>
> b) That person shall not, without that person's consent, be required to give evidence or assist in any other investigation or proceeding other than that which the request relates to.

Paragraph 1 of this article shall cease to apply if that person, being free to leave, has not left the Requesting State within a period of [15] consecutive days after having been officially notified that his or her presence is no longer required or, having left, has voluntarily returned.

A person who does not consent to a request pursuant to article 13 or accept an invitation pursuant to article 14 shall not, by reason thereof, be liable to any penalty or subjected to any coercive measure.

Article 16
Provision of publicly available
documents and other records

The Requested State shall provide copies of documents and records in so far as they are open to public access as part of a public register.

The Requested State may provide copies of any other document or record under the same conditions as they would be provided to its own law enforcement and judicial authorities.

Article 17
Search and seizure

The Requested State shall, in so far as its law permits, carry out requests for search and seizure and delivery of any material to the

Requesting State for evidentiary purposes, provided that the rights of bona fide third parties are protected.

Article 18
Certification and authentication

A request for assistance shall not require certification or authentication.

Article 19
Costs

The ordinary costs of executing a request shall be borne by the Requested State, unless otherwise determined. The Parties shall consult in advance to determine the terms and conditions under which costs of a substantial or extraordinary nature will be borne.

Article 20
Consultation

The Parties shall consult promptly, at the request of either, concerning the interpretation and application of this Treaty.

Article 21
Final provisions

This Treaty is subject to (ratification, acceptance or approval).

This Treaty shall enter into force on the thirtieth day after the instruments of (ratification, acceptance or approval) are exchanged.

This Treaty shall apply to requests made after its entry into force, even if the relevant acts or omissions occurred prior to that date.

Either Party may denounce this Treaty by giving notice in writing to the other Party. Such denunciation shall take effect six months following the date on which notice is received by the other Party.

Model Treaty on the Transfer of Proceedings in Criminal Matters

Adopted by the General Assembly as resolution 45/118 on the recommendation of the Eighth Congress

Article 1
Scope of application

When a person is suspected of having committed an offence under the law of a State which is a Contracting Party, the State may request another State which is a Contracting Party to take proceedings in respect of this offence.

The Contracting Parties shall take necessary legislative measures to ensure the necessary jurisdictions upon a request to take proceedings.

Article 2
Channels of communications

A request to take proceedings shall be made in writing. The request, supporting documents and subsequent communications shall be transmitted throught diplomatic channels, directly between the ministries of justice or any other designated authorities.

Article 3
Required documents

The request shall contain or be accompanied by the following information:

a) The authority presenting the request;

b) A description of the act for which transfer of proceedings is being requested, including time and place of the offence;

c) A statement on the results of investigations substantiating suspicion of an offence;

d) The legal provisions by which the act is considered an offence;

e) A statement on the identity, nationality and residence of the suspected person.

The documents shall be accompanied by a translation into the language of the Requested State or into another language acceptable to that State.

Article 4
Certification and authentication

A request to take proceedings shall not require certification or authentication.

Article 5
Decision on the request

The competent authorities of the Requested State shall examine what action to take on the request and shall promptly communicate their decision.

Article 6
Dual criminality

A request to take proceedings can be complied with only if the act on which the request is based would be an offence if committed in the territory of the Requested State.

Article 7
Grounds for refusal

The Requested State shall communicate reasons for refusal of a request to take proceedings. Acceptance may be refused if:

a) The suspected person is not a national of or ordinary resident in the Requested State;

b) The act is an offence under military law, and not also an offence under ordinary criminal law;

c) The offence is in connection with taxes, duties, customs or exchange;

d) The offence is regarded by the Requested State as being of a political nature.

Article 8
The position of the suspected person

The suspected person may express to either State his or her interest in the transfer of the proceedings. Such interest may also be expressed by the legal representative or close relatives of the suspected person.

Before a request for transfer of proceedings is made, the Requesting State shall, if practicable, allow the suspected person to present his or her views on the alleged offence and the intended transfer.

Article 9
The rights of the victim

The rights of the victim of the offence, in particular his or her right to restitution or compensation, are not to be affected as a result of the transfer. If a settlement of the victim's claim has not been reached before the transfer, the Requested State shall permit representation of the claim in the transferred proceedings, if its law provides for such a possibility. In the event of the death of the victim, these provisions shall apply to his or her dependants accordingly.

Article 10
Effects of the transfer of proceedings
on the Requesting State

Upon acceptance by the Requested State of the request to take proceedings against the suspected person, the Requesting State shall provisionally discontinue prosecution, except necessary investigation, including judicial assistance to the Requested State, until informed that the case has finally been disposed of. From that date on, the Requesting State shall definitely refrain from further prosecution of the same offence.

Article 11
Effects of the transfer of proceedings
on the Requested State

The proceedings shall be governed by the law of the Requested State. When charging the suspected person under its law, the Requested State shall make the necessary adjustment with respect to particular elements in the legal description of the offence.

As far as compatible with the law of the Requested State, any act performed in the Requesting State shall have the same validity in the Requested State.

The Requested State shall inform the Requesting State of the decision taken as a result of the proceedings.

Article 12
Provisional measures

When the Requesting State requests transfer of proceedings, the Requested State may apply all provisional measures, including provisional detention and seizure, as could be applied under its own law if the offence had been committed in its territory.

Article 13
The plurality of criminal proceedings

When criminal proceedings are pending in two or more States against the same suspected person for the same offence, the States shall conduct consultations to decide which of them should continue the proceedings.

Article 14
Costs

Any costs incurred by a Contracting Party because of a transfer of proceedings shall not be refunded, unless otherwise agreed by both the Requesting and Requested States.

Article 15
Final provisions

This Treaty is subject to (ratification, acceptance or approval).

This Treaty shall enter into force on the thirtieth day after the instruments of ratification are exchanged.

This Treaty shall apply to requests made after its entry into force, even if the relevant acts or omissions occurred prior to that date.

Either Contracting Party may denounce this Treaty by giving notice in writing to the other Party. Such denunciation shall take effect six months following the date on which notice is received by the other Party.

Model Treaty on the Transfer of Supervision of Offenders Conditionally Sentenced or Conditionally Released

Adopted by the General Assembly as resolution 45 /118 on the recommendation of the Eighth Congress

Article 1
Scope of application

This Treaty shall be applicable if, according to a final court decision, a person has been found guilty of an offence and has been:

> a) Placed on probation without sentence having been pronounced;

> b) Given a suspended sentence involving deprivation of liberty;

> c) Given a sentence which has been modified by parole or conditionally suspended.

The State where the decision was taken (sentencing State) may request another State (administering State) to take responsibility for applying the terms of the decision (transfer of supervision).

Article 2
Channels of communications

A request for the transfer of supervision shall be made in writing. The request, supporting documents and subsequent communications shall be transmitted through diplomatic channels, directly between the ministries of justice or any other designated authorities.

Article 3
Required documents

A request for the transfer of supervision shall contain all necessary information on identity, nationality and residence of the sentenced person and be accompanied by any court decision referred to in the preceding provision and a certificate that this decision is final.

The documents shall be accompanied by a translation into the language of the requested State or into another language acceptable to that State.

Article 4
Certification and authentication

A request for the transfer of supervision shall not require certification or authentication.

Article 5
Decision on the request

The competent authorities of the Requested State shall examine what action to take on the request and shall promptly communicate their decision.

Article 6
Dual criminality

A request for the transfer of supervision can be complied with only if the act on which the request is based would be an offence if committed in the territory of the administering State.

Article 7
Grounds for refusal

If the administering State refuses acceptance of a request, it shall communicate the reasons for refusal. Acceptance may be refused where:

a) The sentenced person is not an ordinary resident in the administering State;

b) The act is an offence under military law, and is not also an offence under ordinary criminal law;

c) The offence is in connection with taxes, duties, customs or exchange;

d) The offence is regarded by the administering State as being of a political nature;

e) The administering State, under its own law, can no longer carry out the supervision or enforce the sanction because of lapse of time.

Article 8
The position of the sentenced person

Whether sentenced or standing trial, the sentenced person may express to the sentencing State his or her interest in a transfer of supervision and his or her willingness to fulfil any conditions to be imposed. Such interest may also be expressed by his or her legal representative or close relatives.

Article 9
The rights of the victim

The rights of the victim of the offence, in particular his or her right to restitution or compensation, are not to be affected as a result of the transfer. In the event of the death of the victim, this provision shall apply to his or her dependants accordingly.

Article 10
The effect of the transfer of
supervision on the sentencing State

The acceptance by the administering State of responsibility for applying the terms of the decision shall extinguish the competence of the sentencing State to enforce the sentence.

Article 11
The effects of the transfer of
supervision on the administering State

The supervision transferred upon agreement and the subsequent procedure shall be carried out in accord with the law of the administering State. That State alone shall have the right of revocation. That State may adapt to its own law the conditions or measures prescribed, providing they are not more severe than those pronounced in the sentencing State.

If the administering State revokes the conditional sentence or conditional release, it shall enforce the sentence in accord with its own law without, however, going beyond the limits imposed by the sentencing State.

Article 12
Review, pardon and amnesty

The sentencing State alone shall have the right to decide on any application to reopen the case.

Each Party may grant pardon, amnesty or commutation of the sentence.

Article 13
Information

The Contracting Parties shall keep each other informed, as necessary, of circumstances likely to affect supervision or enforcement in the administering State.

After expiration of the period of supervision, the administering State shall provide to the sentencing State, at its request, a final report on the supervised person's conduct and compliance with the measures imposed.

Article 14
Costs

Supervision and enforcement costs incurred in the administering State shall not be refunded, unless otherwise agreed by both the sentencing State and the administering State.

Article 15
Final provisions

This Treaty is subject to (ratification, acceptance or approval).

This Treaty shall enter into force on the thirtieth day after the instruments of (ratification, acceptance or approval) are exchanged.

This Treaty shall apply to requests made after its entry into force, even if the relevant acts or omissions occurred prior to that date.

Either Party may denounce this Treaty by giving notice in writing to the other Party. Such denunciation shall take effect six months following the date on which notice is received by the other Party.

Model Treaty for the Prevention of Crimes that Infringe on the Cultural Heritage of Peoples in the Form of Movable Property

Adopted by the Eighth Crime Congress
and welcomed by the General Assembly
in resolution 45/121

Article 1
Scope of application and definition

For the purposes of this Treaty, movable cultural property shall be understood as referring to property which, on religious or secular grounds, is specifically designated by a State Party as being subject to export control by reason of its importance for archaeology, prehistory, history, literature, art or science, and as belonging to one or more of the following categories:

a) Rare collections and specimens of fauna, flora, minerals and anatomy, and objects of paleontological interest;

b) Property relating to history, including the history of science and technology, military history, and the history of societies and religions, as well as to the lives of leaders, thinkers, scientists and artists, and to events of national importance;

c) Products of archaeological excavations or discoveries, including clandestine excavations or discoveries, whether on land or under water;

d) Elements of artistic or historical monuments or archaeological sites which have been dismantled;

e) Antiquities, including tools, ceramics, ornaments, musical instruments, pottery, inscriptions, coins, engraved seals, jewels, weapons and funerary remains;

f) Materials of anthropological, historical or ethnological interest;

g) Property of artistic interest, including paintings, statues, prints and assemblages;

h) Rare manuscripts and incunabula, old books, documents and publications of special interest;

i) Postage and revenue stamps;

j) Phonographic, photographic and cinematographic archives;

k) Articles of furniture and musical instruments of more than 100 years of age.

This Treaty applies to movable cultural property stolen in or illicitly exported from the other State Party after the coming into force of the Treaty.

Article 2
General principles

Each State Party undertakes:

a) To take necessary measures to prohibit the import and export of movable cultural property

    (i) which has been stolen in the other State Party or

    (ii) which has been illicitly exported from the other State Party;

b) To take the necessary measures to prohibit the acquisition of, and dealing within its territory with, movable cultural property which has been imported contrary to the above prohibitions;

c) To legislate to prevent persons and institutions within its territory from entering into international conspiracies with respect to movable cultural property;

d) To provide information concerning stolen movable cultural property to an international data base agreed upon between the States Parties;

e) To take measures to ensure that the purchaser of stolen movable cultural property which is listed on the international data base is not considered to have purchased such property in good faith;

f) To introduce a system whereby the export of movable cultural property is authorized by issue of an export certificate;

g) To use all means, including the fostering of public awareness, to combat illicit import and export, theft, illicit excavations and illicit dealing in movable cultural property.

Each State undertakes to take the necessary measures to recover and return, at the request of the other State Party, any movable cultural property which is covered in subparagraph a) above.

Article 3
Sanctions

Each State Party undertakes to impose sanctions upon:

a) Persons or institutions responsible for illicit import or export of movable cultural property;

b) Persons or institutions that knowingly acquire or deal in stolen or illicitly imported movable cultural property;

c) Persons or institutions that enter into international conspiracies to obtain, export or import movable cultural property by illicit means.

Article 4
Procedures

Requests for recovery and return shall be made through diplomatic channels.

All expenses incidental to the return and delivery of the movable cultural property shall be borne by the requesting State Party, and no persons or institution shall be entitled to claim any form of compensation from the State Party returning the property claimed. Neither shall the requesting State Party be required to compensate in any way such persons or institutions as may have participated in illegally sending abroad the property in question, although it must pay fair compensation to any person or institution that in good faith acquired or was in legal possession of the property.

Both parties agree not to levy any customs or other duties on such movable property as may be discovered and returned in accord with the present Treaty.

The State Parties agree to make available to each other information to assist in combating crimes against movable cultural property.

Each State Party shall provide information concerning laws which protect its movable cultural property to an international data base agreed upon between the States Parties.

Article 5
Final provisions

This Treaty is subject to (ratification, acceptance or approval).

This Treaty shall enter into force on the thirtieth day after the instruments of (ratification, acceptance or approval) are exchanged.

Either State Party may denounce this Treaty by giving notice in writing to the other State Party. Such denunciation shall take effect six months following the date on which notice is received by the other State Party.

This treaty is intended to be complementary to, and does not in any way exclude, participation in other international arrangements.

Annex to Resolution on Measures Against International Terrorism
Approved by the Eighth Congress

Definition
It would be useful to identify behaviour that the international community regards as unacceptable and that requires the application of effective preventive and repressive measures consistent with international law, although to date the international community has been unable to arrive at a universally agreed meaning of what is included in the term "international terrorism".

Identification of the problems
Existing international norms may not be sufficient to control terrorist violence. Among the issues of concern are: State policies and practices that may be considered a violation of international treaty obligations; the absence of specific norms on State responsibility to carry out international obligations; abuse of diplomat-

ic immunity; the absence of norms concerning acts of States not prohibited by international law; the absence of international regulation and control of traffic in arms; the inadequacy of international mechanisms for the peaceful resolution of conflicts and protection of human rights; the lack of universal acceptance of the principle of aut dedere aut iudicare; and the shortcoming of international cooperation in preventing and controlling terrorist violence.

International cooperation for the effective and uniform prevention and control of terrorism

Effective measures to be developed include: cooperation between law enforcement agencies, prosecutors and the judiciary; integration of the various agencies responsible for law enforcement and criminal justice; inter-State cooperation in penal matters; education and training of law enforcement personnel; and educational and public awareness programmes through the mass media.

Jurisdiction

Greater uniformity in the laws and practices of States concerning criminal jurisdiction should be encouraged, while over-extension of national jurisdiction is avoided to prevent legal conflicts between States. Jurisdictional priorities should give territoriality the first priority.

Extradition

States should develop and implement effective international extradition treaties. The political offence exception should not be a bar to extradition for crimes of terrorist violence, except when the requested State submits the case to its competent authorities for prosecution or transfers the case to another State for prosecution.

Mutual assistance and cooperation

Prevention and control of terrorist violence depends on mutual cooperation between States in securing evidence for prosecution or extradition of the offenders. States should also lend each other assistance in penal matters.

Non-applicability of defence

Defence based on obedience to superior orders or acts of State should not apply with respect to persons who have violated international conventions against terrorist violence.

Conduct of States

Terrorist violence supported, carried out or acquiesced to by States should be more effectively curbed by the international community, and the United Nations should develop mechanisms for the control of such conduct.

Targets of vulnerability

The feasibility of an international convention to protect targets that are particularly vulnerable, the destruction of which would cause great harm to populations or society, such as hydroelectric or nuclear facilities, should be studied.

Control of weapons, ammunition and explosives

States should develop national legislation for the control of weapons, ammunition and explosives that may be used for terrorist purposes. International regulations on the transfer, import, export and storage of such should be harmonized.

Protection of the judiciary and of criminal justice personnel

States should adopt measures to protect the judiciary, criminal justice personnel, jurors and lawyers involved in trials of terrorism cases.

Protection of victims

States should establish measures for the protection, assistance and relief of victims of terrorism.

Protection of witnesses

States should adopt measures to protect witnesses of terrorist acts.

Treatment of offenders

States should diminsh existing disparities in the sentencing of terrorist offenders. Persons charged with or convicted of terrorist offences must be treated without discrimination and in accord with internationally recognized human rights standards.

Role of the mass media

States and the mass media should consider guidelines to control the following: sensationalizing and justifying terrorist violence; disseminating strategic information on potential targets; and disseminating tactical information while terrorist acts are taking place. These guidelines are in no way intended to restrict the basic human right of freedom of speech or to encourage interference in the domestic affairs of other States.

Codification of international criminal law and creation of an international criminal court

The International Law Commission should be encouraged to continue to explore the possibility of an international criminal court or some other international mechanism to have jurisdiction over persons who have committed offences, including those connected with terrorism or illicit trafficking in drugs. States could also explore the possibility of separate international criminal courts of regional or subregional jurisdiction in which grave international crimes could be brought to trial and the incorporation of such courts within the United Nations system.

Enhancing the effectiveness of international cooperation

States that are signatories to international conventions prohibiting terrorist violence are urged to ratify those conventions and enforce their provisions, and States that are not signatories are urged to ratify and enforce those conventions. The central role of the United Nations, its Crime Prevention and Criminal Justice Branch and the Centre for Social Development and Humanitarian Affairs of the United Nations Office at Vienna should be strengthened in order to preserve peace, strengthen the world order and fight against crime under the rule of law.

Statement of Principles and Programme of Action of the United Nations Crime Prevention and Criminal Justice Programme

Adopted November 1991 at the Versailles Minsterial Conference and approved by the General Assembly as an annex to resolution 46/152, which replaced the Committee on Crime Prevention and Control with the Commission on Crime Prevention and Criminal Justice and set the guidelines for its work.

Goals and scope of the Commission's programme of work

The Commission is to: contribute to the prevention of crime within and among States; the control of crime both nationally and internationally; the strengthening of regional and international cooperation in crime prevention, criminal justice and the combating of transnational crime; the integration and consolidation of the efforts of States in preventing and combating transnational crime; more efficient and effective administration of justice, with due respect for the human rights of those affected by crime and all those involved in the criminal justice system; and the promotion of the highest standards of fairness, humanity, justice and professional conduct.

The programme is to include: research and studies at the national, regional and global levels on specific prevention issues and criminal justice measures; regular international surveys for the assessment of trends in crime and of developments in the operation of criminal justice systems and crime prevention strategies; exchange and dissemination of information among States, particularly with regard to innovative measures; training and upgrading the skills of personnel working in the various areas of crime prevention and criminal justice; and technical assistance, including advisory services, particularly in respect of the planning, implementation and evaluation of crime prevention and criminal justice programmes, training and the use of modern communication and information techniques.

Special attention shall be paid to the creation of mechanisms for flexible and appropriate assistance and response to the needs of Member States at their request, without duplication of the activities of other existing mechanisms.

Priority areas

Priorities are to be determined in response to the States' needs and concerns, with particular consideration given to empirical evidence, including research findings and other information on the nature, extent and trends of crime control on all levels; the needs of developing or developed countries confronting specific difficulties related to national or international circumstances; the need for balance between programme development and practical action; the protection of human rights in the administration of justice and the prevention and control of crime; the assessment of areas in which concerted action at the international level and within the framework of the United Nations programme would be most effective; and avoidance of overlapping with the activities of other elements of the United Nations system or of other entities.

Structure and management

The Commission will consist of 40 United Nations Member States elected for three-year terms by the Economic and Social Council on the basis of the principle of equitable geographical distribution. The Commission will hold annual sessions of not more than 10 working days.

The Commission will: provide policy guidance to the United Nations in the field of crime prevention and criminal justice; develop, monitor and review the implementation of the programme on the basis of a system of medium-term planning; help coordinate activities of regional and interregional institutes; mobilize support of Member States for the programme; and prepare the Congresses on the Prevention of Crime and the Treatment of Offenders and consider topics suggested by those congresses.

When necessary, the Commission will employ the services of a limited number of qualified and experienced experts, whether as individual consultants or in working groups.

In regard to the organizational structure of the Secretariat and of the programme, it is recommended to the Secretary-General that an upgrading of the Crime Prevention and Criminal Justice Branch into a division should be effected as soon as possible, within the framework of the total available resources of the United Nations.

Crime Congresses

The United Nations crime congresses will provide for the exchange of views between States, intergovernmental and non-governmental organizations, and individuals representing various disciplines; the exchange of experiences in research, law and policy development; and the identification of emerging trends and issues in crime prevention and criminal justice. They will also offer advice to the Commission on its work programme.

Congresses are to be held every five years, for a period of between five and 10 working days. The Commission will select precisely defined topics for the congresses so as to ensure a focussed and productive discussion.

Programme support

The activities of the United Nations interregional and regional institutes for the prevention of crime and the treatment of offenders should be supported by Member States and the United Nations, with particular attention to the needs of the institutes located in developing countries. The institutes shall keep one another and the Commission informed of their programme of work and its implementation, and the Commission will seek to mobilize extrabudgetary support for their activities.

Member States should support the United Nations in the development and maintenance of the global crime and justice information network in order to facilitate the collection, analysis, exchange and dissemination, as appropriate, of information and the centralization of inputs from non-governmental organizations and scientific institutions in the crime field. States should also provide the Secretary-General with data on the dynamics, structure and extent of crime and of the operation of crime prevention and criminal justice strategies in their respective countries.

The programme should be funded from the regular budget of the United Nations. Funds allocated for technical assistance may be supplemented by direct voluntary contributions from Member States and interested funding agencies. Member States are encouraged to contribute to the United Nations Crime Prevention and Criminal Justice Fund. They also are encouraged to contribute in kind for the operational activities of the programme, particularly by seconding staff, organizing training courses and seminars and providing requisite equipment and services.

Statement of Principles

States should translate their political will into concrete action by committing themselves to provide, among other things, a framework for inter-State cooperation in combating serious new forms and transnational aspects of crime; the means of assistance, particularly to developing countries, for more effective crime prevention and more humane criminal justice; and adequate resources to operate an effective United Nations crime programme.

Notwithstanding the fact that the world is experiencing very important changes resulting in a political climate conducive to democracy, to international cooperation, and to more widespread enjoyment of basic human rights and fundamental freedoms, the world today remains beset by violence and other forms of serious crime—phenomena which constitute a threat to the rule of law.

Further, justice based on the rule of law is the pillar on which civilized society rests, and States should seek to improve its quality. The lowering of the world crime rate is related to, among other factors, the improvement of the social conditions of the population, while rising crime impairs the process of development and the general well-being of humanity.

The growing internationalization of crime must be met by new and commensurate resources. Democracy and a better quality of life can flourish only in a context of peace, and crime poses a threat to stability and a safe environment.

Finally, the international community should increase its support of technical cooperation and assistance activities for the benefit of all countries and acknowledge the contribution of the United Nations crime prevention and criminal justice programme to the international community.

Naples Political Declaration and Global Action Plan

Adopted 23 November 1994, by the World Ministerial Conference on Transnational Crime, in Naples, Italy, and approved by General Assembly Resolution 49/159; text contained in A/49/748.

I Political Declaration

Conference participants resolve to protect their societies from organized crime in all its forms through strict and effective legislative measures and operational instruments, always consistent with internationally recognized human rights and fundamental freedoms. The fight against organized crime should be accorded high priority by States and by all relevant global and regional organizations, with the necessary support of the general public, the media, business, institutions and non-governmental organizations. Transnational crime threatens the social and economic growth of developing countries and countries in transition, and the international community should assist these countries in their efforts to strengthen criminal justice institutions. States which have not yet become party to the UN Convention against Illicit Traffic in Narcotic Drugs and Psychotropic Substances of 1988 are urged to do so.

More effective international cooperation is needed, especially in relation to:

- Closer alignment of legislative texts concerning organized crime;

- Operational matters at the investigative, prosecutorial and jusicial levels;

- Establishing modalities and basic principles for international cooperation at the regional and global levels;

- Measures and strategies to prevent and combat money-laundering and to control the use of the proceeds of crime.

II Global action plan against organized transnational crime

Problems and dangers posed by organized crime

If organized crime is not resisted, it will undermine political structures, endanger internal peace and social and economic development, and threaten not only emerging democracies, but also States with well-established democratic traditions.

The international community is urged to adopt a generally agreed concept of organized crime as a basis for more compatible national responses and more effective international cooperation. To recognize and intelligently to prevent and combat organized transnational crime, the international community should increase its knowledge of criminal organizations and their dynamics. States should collect, analyse and disseminate reliable statistics and information on the phenomenon.

Strengthening national legislation

Objectives for national legislation directed against organized transnational crime include improved investigative measures, penal codes and anti-corruption safeguards. Substantive legislation penalizing participation in criminal association or conspiracies and imposing criminal liability on corporate bodies should be considered, when necessary, as a means of strengthening capabilities to combat organized crime. States should ensure they possess structures and capabilities throughout their entire criminal justice system adequate to deal with complex organized criminal activities. States should endeavour, when warranted, to establish and equip special investigative units with expertise in the nature and methods of organized criminal groups.

International cooperation

States are enjoined to implement fully existing bilateral and multilateral conventions and agreements concerning extradition, to ensure that all provisions are respected and that there is effective implementation of requests for mutual legal assistance. States should ensure that they have in place the basic components of a functional system of international cooperation, given the ability of organized transnational crime to shift its operations from country to country and to widen the magnitude of its activities. They should also improve the practical application of existing agreements through informal and operational mechanisms and improve basic intelligence-gathering capability, while respecting individual rights and freedoms.

Feasibility of international instruments

The Commission on Crime Prevention and Criminal Justice is to request the views of governments on the impact of an international convention on organized crime and the issues it might cover.

States are asked to consider the practical aspects of establishing more effective tools and instruments, such as model technical agreements, manuals for police and judicial cooperation, methods for the regular flow of information as well as information databases. Such instruments might be introduced as memoranda of understanding similar to those already concluded by some States in the field of international drug-trafficking.

Control of money-laundering

The fight against organized transnational crime should be based on strategies aimed at defeating the economic power of criminal organizations. States should ensure that the fight involves both criminal law measures, particularly those pertaining to sanctioning and sentencing, and adequate regulatory mechanisms. States should also consider making it a criminal offence to launder the proceeds of criminal activities, given that criminal groups accumulate large amounts of capital and need to launder them and invest in legitimate businesses.

States should consider adopting legislative and regulatory measures limiting financial secrecy. These measures should include application of the "know your customer" rule, as well as the reporting of suspicious financial transactions, while protecting financial institutions from liability except in cases of gross negligence. States should also identify businesses which may serve as money launderers and determine the feasibility of extending reporting and other requirements to areas other than banking and finance. The United Nations and other international and regional organizations should reinforce common regulatory and enforcement strategies in this regard.

States should consider adopting legislative measures to confiscate or seize illicit proceeds, as well as utilizing provisional arrangements, such as the freezing or seizing of assets, with due respect for bona fide third parties. Subject to the principles of their legal systems, States should consider sharing forfeited assets and, under specific conditions, of confiscating illicit proceeds without a criminal conviction, or confiscating or seizing sums higher than those relating to the crime for which judgement has been passed.

States should also consider preventive measures ensuring the identification of owners of companies and accurate information on acquisitions and transfers and high ethical standards in public administration, as well as measures ensuring cooperation between financial regulatory authorities and those applying penal laws.

The United Nations should provide technical assistance to countries on request, using the expertise of all its relevant institutes and agencies, including the International Scientific and Professional Advisory Council.

Support for the United Nations
Crime Prevention Programme

Existing resources not being sufficient for the United Nations crime prevention and criminal justice programme to carry out its responsibilities, a higher priority should be accorded to United Nations crime control activities by allocating adequate resources in the medium-term plan for 1992-1997 and in corresponding biennial budgets. States should also increase their voluntary contributions to the programme in order to strengthen the United Nations crime control structure.

Task Force

Appreciation is expressed to the Government of Italy for its offer to organize and host, at no cost to the United Nations, an international task force to study the feasibility of establishing an international training centre for law enforcement and criminal justice personnel.

Since its foundation, the United Nations, drawing on the principles of the Charter and the International Bill of Human Rights, has formulated numerous international instruments in crime prevention and criminal justice. The full texts of such instruments are contained in the Compendium of United Nations Standards and Norms in Crime Prevention and Criminal Justice *(United Nations Publication, Sales No. E.92.IV.1, ISBN 92-1-130148-3).*

Stop Crime